Hemispheres 1

Scott Cameron
Mari Vargo

Susan Iannuzzi
Consultant

Jenny Bixby
Contributor, Expansion Units

McGraw-Hill ELT

Hemispheres 1 Student Book

Published by McGraw-Hill ESL/ELT, a business unit of The McGraw-Hill Companies, Inc., 1221 Avenue of the Americas, New York, NY 10020.

ISBN 13: 978-0-07-719105-4 (Student Book with Audio Highlights)
ISBN 10: 0-07-719105-6
1 2 3 4 5 6 7 8 9 10 QWC 11 10 09 08 07

Editorial director: Tina Carver
Series editor: Annie Sullivan
Senior development editors: Terre Passero, Annie Sullivan
Production manager: Juanita Thompson
Production coordinator: James D. Gwyn
Cover Designer: Wee Design Group
Reading and chart designs: Cynthia Malaran
Interior designer: Nesbitt Graphics, Inc.
Artists: Mona Daly; Sylvie Pinsonneaux; Nadia Simard
Photo researcher: Photoquick Research

The credits section for this book begins on page 142 and is considered an extension of the copyright page.

Cover photo: © Farinaz Taghavi/Corbis

Hemispheres 1 Components

Student Book with Audio Highlights
Workbook
Teacher's Manual
Audio CDs
DVD
DVD Workbook
Online Learning Center
EZ Test® CD-ROM Test Generator
Teacher Training DVD

www.esl.mcgraw-hill.com

The *McGraw·Hill* Companies

ACKNOWLEDGMENTS

The authors and publisher would like thank the following teachers, program directors, and teacher trainers, who reviewed the Hemispheres program at various stages of development and whose comments, reviews, and field-testing were instrumental in helping us shape the series:

Dee Parker, Jeffrey Taschner, **American University Alumni Language Center,** Bangkok, Thailand

David Scholz, **AUA- Rajadamri Branch,** Bangkok, Thailand

Snow White O. Smelser, **AUA- Ratchayothin,** Bangkok, Thailand

Anthony Pavia, Dr. Joseph W. Southern, **AUA-Srinikarin,** Bangkok, Thailand

Maria Adele Ryan, Maria Teresa de la Torre Aranda, **Associação Alumni,** São Paulo, Brazil

Lúcia Catharina Bodeman Campos, **Associação Brasil-América (ABA),** Pernambuco, Brazil

Marissa Araquistain, Gabriel Areas, Douglas Arroliga, Francisco Hodgson, Maria Mora, Aleyda Reyes, Jairo Rivar, Gloria Tunnerman, Sarah Walsh, **Ave Maria College of the Americas,** Managua, Nicaragua

Bruce Avasadanand, **Bangkok School of Management,** Bangkok, Thailand

Yanan Une-aree, **Bangkok University,** Bangkok, Thailand

Suchada Rattanawanitpun, **Burapha University,** Chon Buri, Thailand

Isabela de Freitas Villas Boas, Catherine Taliaferro Cox, **Casa Thomas Jefferson,** Brasilia, Brazil

Fernando Trevino, **Centro de Idiomas,** Monterrey, Mexico

Maria Zavala, **Centro Educativo los Pinos,** Guadalajara, Mexico

Karen Pereira Meneses, **Centro Educativo Yurusti,** Costa Rica

Wuyen Wayne Ni, **Chung Kuo Institute of Technology and Commerce,** Taipei, Taiwan

Mónica González, **Colegio InterCanadiense de Puebla,** A.C, Puebla, Mexico

Rosa Ma. Chacon, Henry Angulo Jiménez, Johannia Piedra, **Colegio Saleciano Don Bosco,** San Jose, Costa Rica

Marjorie Friedman, **ELS Language Centers,** Florida, United States

Joseph Dziver, **Florida State University** - English Language Program, Panama

Raymond Kao, **Fu Hsing Kang College,** Taipei, Taiwan

Marie J. Guilloteaux, **Gyeongsang National University,** Jinju, Korea

Jana Opicic, **Harvest English Institute,** New Jersey, United States

Wilma Luth, **Hokusei Gakuen University,** Sapporo, Japan

Daniela Alves Meyer, José Manuel da Silva, Maria do Socorro Guimarães, **Instituto Brasil-Estados Unidos (IBEU),** Rio de Janeiro, Brazil

Rosario Garcia Alfonso, **Instituto Copernico,** Guadalajara, Mexico

Nefertiti Gonzales, **Instituto Mexicano Madero,** Puebla, Mexico

Rosa Isabel de la Garza, Elvira Marroquin Medina, **Instituto Regiomontano,** Monterrey, Mexico

Robert van Trieste, **Inter American University of Puerto Rico,** San Juan, Puerto Rico

Elisabeth Lindgren, Annetta Stroud, **Intrax International Institute,** California, United States

Tracy Cramer, **Kansai Gaidai University,** Osaska, Japan

Lilliam Quesada Solano, **Licco Experimental Bilingue Jose Figueres,** Cartago, Costa Rica

Paul Cameron, **National Chengchi University,** Taipei, Taiwan

Elsa Fan, **National Chiao Tung University,** Taipei, Taiwan

Jessie Huang, **National Central University,** Taipei, Taiwan

Marcia Monica A. Saiz, **Naval Academy,** Brazil

Pamela Vittorio, **New School University,** New York, United States

Steve Cornwell, **Osaka Jogakuin College,** Osaska, Japan

Kathryn Aparicio, Inda Shirley, **San Francisco Institute of English,** California, United States

Dan Neal, **Shih Chien University,** Taipei, Taiwan

Kevin Miller, **Shikoku University,** Tokushima, Japan

Mark Brown, Linda Sky Emerson, Jinyoung Hong, Young-Ok Kim, **Sogang University,** Seoul, Korea

Colin Gullberg, **Soochow University,** Taipei, Taiwan

Michael Martin, Juthumas Sukontha, **Sripatum University,** Bangkok, Thailand

Damian Benstead, Roy Langdon, **Sungkyunkwan University,** Seoul, Korea

Cheryl Magnant, Jeff Moore, Devon Scoble, **Sungkyunkwan University,** Seoul, Korea

Raymond Kao, Taiwan **Military University,** Taipei, Taiwan

Dr. Saneh Thongrin, **Thammasat University,** Bangkok, Thailand

Patrick Kiernan, **Tokyo Denki University,** Tokyo, Japan

Yoshiko Matsubayashi, **Tokyo International University,** Saitama, Japan

Mike Hood, Patrick McCoy, **Tokyo University,** Tokyo, Japan

Rafael Cárdenas, Victoria Peralta, Isaac Secaida, Roy Tejeira, **UDELAS - Centro Inteligente de Lenguas de Las Américas,** Panama

Olga Chaves Carballo, **ULACIT,** San Jose, Costa Rica

Adela de Maria y Campos, **Unidades Básicas UPAEP,** Puebla, Mexico

Olda C. de Arauz, **Universidad Autonoma de Chiriqui,** Panama

Ignacio Yepez, **Universidad Autonoma de Guadalajara,** Guadalajara, Mexico

Yohanna Abarca Amador, Cesar Navas Brenes, Gabriela Cerdas, Elisa Li Chan, Ligia de Coto, Maria Eugenia Flores, Carlos Navarro, Johanna Piedra, Allen Quesada-Pacheco, Mary Scholl, Karen Solis, Alonso Canales Viquez, **Universidad de Costa Rica,** San Jose, Costa Rica

John Ball, Geraldine Torack-Durán, **Universidad de las Americas, A.C.,** Mexico City, Mexico

Victoria Lee, **Universidad del Istmo,** Panama

Ramiro Padilla Muñoz, Sandra Hernandez Salazar, **Universidad del Valle de Atemajac (UNIVA),** Guadalajara, Mexico

Alan Heaberlin, Sophia Holder, **Universidad Interamericana,** San Jose, Costa Rica

Fraser Smith, Michael Werner, **Universidad Latina,** Costa Rica

Gilberto Hernàndez, **Universidad Metropolitana Castro Carazo,** Alajuela, Costa Rica

Angela Calderon, **Universidad Santa Maria La Antigua,** Panama

Edith Espino, **Universidad Tecnológica de Panamá,** Panama

Thomas Riedmiller, **University of Northern Iowa,** Iowa, United States

Stella M. Aneiro, Ivette Delgado, Prof. Marisol Santiago Pérez , Ida Roman, **University of Puerto Rico - Arecibo,** Puerto Rico

Aida Caceres, **University of Puerto Rico - Humacao,** Humacao, Puerto Rico

Regino Megill, **University of Puerto Rico - Ponce,** Ponce, Puerto Rico

Dr. Emily Krasinski, **University of Puerto Rico,** San Juan, Puerto Rico

WELCOME TO HEMISPHERES

Hemispheres puts skills-building back into integrated skills. Hemispheres is a four-level integrated skills series for adults and young adults that takes students from high beginning to high intermediate level. The course is uniquely suitable for students studying general English language and those studying English with a view toward more academic work. The series strategically develops both language skills and critical thinking skills. The thought-provoking topics and appealing, user-friendly design invite learners into the skills development without hesitation.

FEATURES

- **Balance of language areas:** Reading, listening, speaking, writing, and grammar are balanced and integrated throughout the unit.

- **Academic skills:** A variety of activities ensures the purposeful development of academic skills, such as summarizing, paraphrasing, making predictions, identifying gist, and using graphs to aid comprehension.

- **Critical thinking skills:** The consistent focus on essential critical thinking skills, such as analyzing, synthesizing, making inferences, understanding organization, and drawing conclusions, encourages independent thinking and learning.

- **TOEFL® iBT:** Each unit helps to build readiness for the TOEFL® iBT. This section includes a new reading and listening and TOEFL® iBT type questions that include personal interpretation, independent speaking and writing, and integrated speaking and writing.

- **Vocabulary expansion activities:** Additional vocabulary practice activities for each unit reinforce learning.

- **High interest content:** Unusual, attention-grabbing topics generate discussion and personalization.

- **DVD and DVD Workbook:** The DVD illustrates conversation strategies and critical thinking skills in an engaging storyline, and the accompanying DVD Workbook ensures comprehension and encourages more open-ended application of the critical thinking skills.

- **Student book with audio highlights:** Students can listen to dialogues multiple times with the audio for additional individual practice.

- **Recycling:** Content and language are continuously and consistently recycled with variations to lead the learner from receptive to creative language production.

COMPONENTS FOR LEVEL 1

- **Student Book with audio highlights**
- **Interleaved Teacher's Manual**
- **Workbook**
- **Audio CDs**
- **DVD**

- **DVD Workbook**
- **Online Learning Center**
- **EZ Test® CD-ROM with Test Generator**
- **Teacher Training DVD**

*TOEFL is a registered trademark of Educational Testing Service (ETS).
This publication is not endorsed or approved by ETS.

PUTTING THE SKILLS BACK INTO THE FOUR-SKILLS COURSE

Hemispheres has put the skills-building back into the four-skills course. It supports students in the development of language skills, while at the same time emphasizing critical thinking skills. Reading, listening, speaking, and writing skills are purposefully developed in ways that are similar to single skill books. Helpful skill focus boxes make the skills development information manageable and give students practical guidance that they can use throughout the book or as a reference.

Critical Thinking Skills

Hemispheres features critical thinking skills development together with language skills development. Students are encouraged to take charge of their learning and to become independent thinkers. Activities ask students to make inferences, analyze, synthesize, and understand the relationships between ideas.

Integrating the Skills

Hemispheres carefully integrates skills in both presentations and practice. Meaningful speaking activities and role-plays are integrated with reading and listening. Relevant reading models are integrated with writing. Grammar is practiced through thematically related reading, listening, speaking, and writing. Natural personalization opportunities feature throughout the series.

Putting It Together and TOEFL® iBT

Hemispheres builds valuable test taking skills while recycling critical thinking skills in the Putting It Together section of each unit. A strategic pairing of reading and listening requires students analyze or synthesize information to understand how the two are related. The reading may present a theory, while the listening provides examples supporting that theory; the reading may explain a problem, while the listening provides a solution to the problem; the reading may present an argument, while the listening presents a counterargument; or the reading and listening may present different points of view. The readings and listenings are short and thematically related to the unit, and they are followed by comprehension checkpoints. Students are asked non-intimidating TOEFL® iBT style questions to identify the relationship between the ideas in the reading and those in the listening. They then have an opportunity to discuss and personalize the topic in this section.

DVD

Shot in high-definition, the DVD features six young adults who work at the *Hemispheres* internet café. In addition to showing conversation strategies and critical thinking skills in real-life contexts, the DVD recycles the vocabulary and grammar presented in the student books.

Correlations

Hemispheres is correlated to the TOEFL®iBT, TOEIC® examination, and CEF. It is solid preparation for students whose instructional needs are linked to any of these instruments.

SCOPE AND SEQUENCE

Unit	Reading	Listening	Grammar
Unit 1 Tell Me About Yourself page 2	★ Scanning for specific information	■ Listening for general information ■ Listening for specific information	The simple present: ■ Affirmative and negative statements ■ *Yes / no* and *wh-* questions ■ Short answers
Unit 2 Who Wants to Live Forever? page 10	★ Skimming for the main idea ■ Scanning for specific information	■ Listening for frequency ★ Making inferences	■ Adverbs of frequency ■ Time expressions
Unit 3 Where Do You Hang Out? page 18	■ Skimming for the main idea ★ Comparing and contrasting	■ Listening to confirm predictions ★ Making inferences	■ *There is / there are* ■ *Some / any* ■ Count and noncount nouns
Expansion Units 1–3 page 26	★ Identifying main idea ■ Scanning for specific information	■ Listening for frequency ★ Categorizing	
Unit 4 It's a Big Mystery page 30	★ Making predictions from photos ★ Reading to identify sequence	★ Listening and sequencing ■ Listening for specific information	■ The simple past: regular and irregular verbs
Unit 5 These Are a Few of My Favorite Things! page 38	★ Making predictions from titles ★ Distinguishing between fact and opinion	■ Listening for time expressions ★ Categorizing	■ Demonstrative adjectives and pronouns *this, that, these, those, this one, that one*
Unit 6 Great ideas page 46	■ Scanning for specific information ★ Identifying the best summary	■ Listening for specific information ★ Identifying the best summary	Modals for ability: ■ *Can / can't* for present ■ *Could / couldn't* for past
Expansion Units 4–6 page 54	★ Making predictions ■ Identifying main idea ■ Identifying details	■ Listening for details ★ Sequencing	

★ Critical thinking skill

Vocabulary	Conversation Strategy	Writing	TOEFL® iBT Focus
■ Categories favorite foods, interests, kinds of movies, kinds of music	■ Asking for clarification	■ Writing statements and questions ■ Writing an email	■ Comparing and contrasting
■ Phrases with *get, take, go* *a lot of sleep, a vacation, exercise, night classes, on a picnic, stressed out, to the movies, vitamins*	■ Showing interest	■ Writing topic sentences	■ Making Inferences
■ Public places *antique stores, bars, boathouse, exhibitions, fountains, nightclubs, pink buildings, restaurants, statues, trees*	■ Asking for additional information	■ Using connecting words *and, but,* and *or* ■ Writing about a landmark in your city	■ Categorizing ■ Identifying advantages and disadvantages
■ Collocations with activities *eat at a restaurant, get fresh air, get some exercise, go ice skating, go skiing, go snowboarding, go swimming, have a picnic, listen to the ocean, play volleyball, relax in the sand, sunbathe*	■ Asking and answering questions in simple present ■ Showing interest	■ Writing questions and answers in simple present ■ Writing questions for an interview about vacations	
■ Synonyms *discover, exciting, hoax, mysterious, strange, unusual*	■ Expressing disbelief	■ Using time words to sequence events *first, then, next, after that, finally* ■ Writing about a trip	■ Identifying predictions ■ Ranking
■ Expressions *be crazy about, be here to stay, be worth every penny, cost an arm and a leg, give someone the creeps, take off, turn down*	■ Expressing similar and different opinions	■ Writing concluding sentences	■ Comparing and contrasting ■ Sequencing
■ Technology *cell phone, display, go online, keyboard, recharge, screen, surf, text message, website*	■ Offering, accepting, and declining invitations	■ Writing a summary ■ Writing about disposable cell phones	■ Identifying a problem and a solution
■ About jeans *all the rage, made a fortune, materials, tent, wear out*	■ Talking about personal experiences ■ Expressing disbelief	■ Writing concluding sentences	

SCOPE AND SEQUENCE

Unit	Reading	Listening	Grammar
Unit 7 Good, Better, Best page 58	★ Using a bar graph to aid comprehension ■ Reading for specific information	■ Listening for specific information ★ Recognizing tone	■ Comparative and superlative forms of adjectives
Unit 8 Trends page 66	■ Skimming to identify topics ★ Getting meaning from context	■ Listening for specific information ★ Listening for gist	■ The present continuous *these days*, *nowadays* ■ Modals for requests and permission *would you, can you, could you, may I, can I, could I*
Unit 9 Making Connections page 74	★ Making inferences ★ Reading to identify sequence	■ Listening for specific information ★ Making inferences	■ Expressions of quantity to express a number or an amount *a lot, some, none, a few, a little, any, not any, several, how much, how many*
Expansion Units 7–9 page 82	■ Reading for details ★ Identifying meaning through context	★ Identifying tone ★ Making inferences ■ Listening for details	
Unit 10 Space Tourism page 86	■ Scanning for specific information ★ Paraphrasing	■ Listening for specific information ★ Comparing and contrasting	■ *Be going to* for future plans and intentions
Unit 11 The Power of the Mind page 94	■ Reading for the main idea ★ Using headings to aid comprehension	■ Listening for specific information ★ Sequencing	■ Verb + *to* + verb *like, need, want, have, decide, plan, expect, hope, plan* + infinitive
Unit 12 Success Starts Early page 102	★ Understanding point of view ■ Identifying details that show point of view	★ Making predictions from photos ■ Listening for specific information ★ Summarizing	■ The present perfect with *for* and *since*
Expansion Units 10–12 page 110	■ Identifying the main ideas ■ Making inferences ■ Paraphrasing	★ Summarizing ■ Listening for details	

★ Critical thinking skill

viii

Vocabulary	Conversation Strategy	Writing	TOEFL® iBT Focus
■ Verb and noun collocations with sports and activities *play (golf, the piano), go (golfing, surfing), do (gymnastics, homework), (no verb) box, golf, jog*	■ Expressing excitement and enthusiasm	■ Organizing ideas with a mind map ■ Writing a paragraph using examples	■ Identifying information that contradicts (refutes) an opinion ■ Interpreting a graph
■ Phrasal verbs with *out* and *over* *eat out, figure out, find out, get over, go out, have over, think over, wear out, work out*	■ Asking permission and making requests	■ Writing a descriptive paragraph ■ Describing a trendy place	■ Identifying examples that support a statement
■ Count and noncount nouns *acquaintance, information, news, participant, research, sender, stranger, study, time, work*	■ Asking for and giving opinions	■ Supporting your opinions ■ Writing about an urban legend	■ Identifying support for an opinion
■ About a city *art galleries, climate, culture, livable, residents, sophisticated*	■ Doing a survey about opinions	■ Organizing ideas with a mind map ■ Supporting your opinion with examples	
■ Compound nouns *airline, businessman, crew members, daredevil, hot-air balloon, outer space, space travel, spaceship*	■ Asking for and giving recommendations	■ Paraphrasing ■ Writing a postcard	■ Identifying pros and cons
■ About a study on pain *device, expectations, increase, moderate, particular, severe, signal, weak*	■ Explaining a process *first, then, finally*	■ Writing a paragraph using supporting details ■ Writing about mind over matter	■ Making inferences
■ Antonyms *capable, independent, intelligent, outgoing, motivated, quiet, talented, thoughtful*	■ Asking for and giving advice	■ Identifying goals and steps to accomplish them ■ Writing a paragraph to show sequence of events	■ Recognizing cause and effect
■ About a pop star *choir, competition, encouraged, professional, talented, turning point, unknown*	■ Asking for recommendations and giving recommendations	■ Writing about steps to accomplish a goal	

5 These Are a Few of My Favorite Things!

READING AND SPEAKING

A ▶ Warm up. Discuss these questions in pairs.

1. What are five things that some children collect?
2. What are five things that some adults collect?
3. Do you collect anything? If so, what's in your collection?

TIP **Possessive Adjectives:** *my, your, his, her, its, their, our*
Possessive adjectives show possession or ownership. They also can show a relationship with another person. For example, *He showed **his** collection to **my** father.*

Ω B ▶ Read. Look at the title and the photos in the article. Predict what it is about. Circle a, b, c, or d.

a. a new and expensive shampoo
b. an expensive haircut
c. an odd and expensive collection
d. odd hairstyles

Collecting the Most Valuable Hair in the World

Connecticut businessman John Reznikoff **is crazy about** hair. In fact, he collects it. Reznikoff has a collection of hair from over 120 famous dead people. He has hair from politicians, musicians, and even the actress Marilyn Monroe. Reznikoff got her hair from a doctor. This doctor cared for Monroe's body after she died. Collectible hair can be expensive. Reznikoff paid a lot of money for some of Abraham Lincoln's hair. Lincoln was president of the United States from 1861 to 1865. The hair **cost an arm and a leg**, but Reznikoff said it was **worth every penny**. "That hair is my favorite item," he explained. So when some collectors offered him $50,000 for it, he **turned down** their offer.

Eric Gaines and his brother Mike collect hair from famous writers like Ernest Hemingway. "When we started," Eric said, "nobody else collected hair. Our friends said, 'Your collection **gives us the creeps**.' But now those same people think it's cool."

Hair collecting began to **take off** in the early 1990s. It grows in popularity every day. There are more than 400 hair collectors in the United States today. There are at least 100 hair collectors in other countries.

This strange new hobby **is here to stay**.

38 Unit 5 These Are a Few of My Favorite Things!

C ▶ Read again. Write *Fact* or *Opinion* for each statement.

1. _____ Reznikoff has a collection of hair from over 120 dead people.
2. _____ Hair collecting began to take off in the early 1990s.
3. _____ Abraham Lincoln's expensive hair was worth every penny.
4. _____ Eric and Mike Gaines collect hair from famous writers.
5. _____ Hair collecting is here to stay.

Skill Focus **Fact or Opinion?**
A fact is information that has been proven to be true. An opinion is a judgment or a belief about something; it may or may not be true.

D ▶ Pair work. Discuss your opinions about the article with a partner.

1. Imagine that you collect things from famous people. Which famous people's possessions do you want?
2. What things do your friends and family collect? Which collection is the most interesting? Why?

VOCABULARY Expressions

A ▶ Identify. Match the expressions with their meanings. Write the letters on the lines.

Expressions
1. ____ be crazy about
2. ____ turn down
3. ____ cost an arm and a leg
4. ____ be worth every penny
5. ____ take off
6. ____ give someone the creeps
7. ____ be here to stay

Meaning
a. be very expensive
b. will last a long time
c. reject or refuse
d. make someone uncomfortable
e. like something (someone) very much
f. have sudden success
g. have very good value

B ▶ Pair work. Discuss these questions. Use the idioms above in your answers.

1. The fans in Photo 1 want autographs. Who are they crazy about? Why?
2. Describe someone or something that you are crazy about.
3. The man in Photo 2 is looking at a piece of art. Do you think he will buy it or turn it down?
4. Describe something that is expensive, but is worth every penny.

Photo 1

Photo2

Unit 5 These Are a Few of My Favorite Things! **39**

▶ **WARM UP** activates prior knowledge of the unit theme and introduces the reading context.

▶ **TIP BOXES** provide reminders or useful language to encourage student discussion.

▶ **ENGAGING CONTENT** about real people, places, and ideas captures student interest.

▶ **ACADEMIC AND CRITICAL THINKING SKILLS** encourage independent thinking and learning. Skills include comparing and contrasting, making inferences, summarizing, analyzing, categorizing, and distinguishing between fact and opinion.

▶ **SKILL FOCUS BOXES** give students practical guidance that they can use throughout the book or as a reference.

▶ **VOCABULARY** is presented and practiced in the opening reading of each unit and in expansion activities at the end of the book.

► **GRAMMAR** explanation and examples serve as a reference for students.

► **GUIDED PRACTICE** includes controlled practice of the grammar or an error correction exercise.

► **INTEGRATED LISTENING AND GRAMMAR ACTIVITIES** allow students to experience the grammar in real language through meaningful, thematically related listening activities.

There is / There are with *some* and *any*

In statements, we use *there is* with singular nouns and *there are* with plural nouns.

There is a small zoo in the park.
There are a lot of great restaurants in that neighborhood.

In questions, we use *Is there* with singular nouns and *Are there* with plural nouns.

Is there a good coffee shop in the area? → Yes, there is.
Are there many trees in Central Park? → Yes, there are.

We use *some* with plural nouns in affirmative statements.

There are **some** interesting places to see in Zona Rosa.

We use *any* with plural nouns in general questions and negative statements.

Are there **any** banks in Central Park? → No, there aren't **any** banks in Central Park.

A ► **Practice.** There is one error in each sentence. Circle and correct the error.

1. Is there any cheap restaurants around here?
2. There isn't any trees in that neighborhood. _____
3. There are any really cool places in Zona Rosa. _____
4. There aren't some really delicious things on the menu. _____
5. Are there a post office near here? _____
6. There's any bank on Main Street. _____

Ω B ► **Listen.** Check (✓) True or False about Dae Hak Ro, a popular area in Seoul, Korea.

	True	False
...aren't any good restaurants in Dae Hak Ro.	☐	☐
...a subway stop in the area.	☐	☐
...an is a bar in the area.	☐	☐
...aren't any museums in the area.	☐	☐

...You Hang Out?

A ► **Read.**
1. Underline foods and drinks in the article.

ChikaLicious

Lidia Vasquez is from Mexico, but she lives in New York. She loves New York, especially the variety of restaurants. Her favorite restaurant is called ChikaLicious. There aren't many restaurants like ChikaLicious. It only serves dessert,
5 cheese, and drinks. In fact, there aren't any other foods on the menu. There aren't even many drinks on the menu, only coffee, tea, and wine. "I spend hours at ChikaLicious," Lidia says. "I usually have some coffee, some cheese, and a piece of cake. I know cheese and coffee are strange together. But
10 really, it's delicious. The restaurant is relaxing, too. There are always fresh flowers on the tables, and there are lots of friendly people."

2. **Pair work.** Ask and answer the questions below. Use *there is, there isn't, there are,* or *there aren't* in your answers.

Example: A: Are there many different kinds of food at ChikaLicious?
   B: No, there aren't many kinds of food at ChikaLicious.

1. What's on the menu at ChikaLicious?
2. Why is the ChikaLicious menu unusual?
3. Why does Lidia like this restaurant?
4. Is there anything on the menu that you like or don't like?

B ► **Group work.** Complete the chart with information about you. Then discuss it with your classmates.

Example: A: My favorite place is Disneyland.
   B: Why do you like it?
   A: Well, there are a lot of interesting things to do.
   B: Are there any bars and restaurants?
   A: Well, there are some nice restaurants. There aren't any bars.

My favorite part of town:	My favorite restaurant:	My favorite place: Disneyland
Why I like it:	Why I like it:	Why I like it: There are a lot of interesting things to do.

► **INTEGRATED READING AND GRAMMAR ACTIVITIES** encourage students to actively apply their understanding of the grammar to aid in reading comprehension.

► **FOLLOW UP ACTIVITIES** include pair work and writing to ensure students are confident applying the grammar in all language areas—reading, writing, listening, and speaking.

► **INTERVIEWS AND GROUP WORK** expand students' skills through personalized, communicative activities.

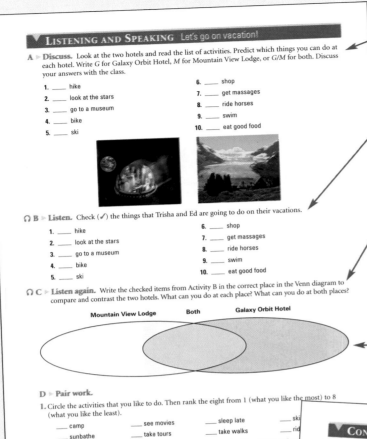

A ▶ Discuss. Look at the two hotels and read the list of activities. Predict which things you can do at each hotel. Write *G* for Galaxy Orbit Hotel, *M* for Mountain View Lodge, or *G/M* for both. Discuss your answers with the class.

1. ____ hike
2. ____ look at the stars
3. ____ go to a museum
4. ____ bike
5. ____ ski

6. ____ shop
7. ____ get massages
8. ____ ride horses
9. ____ swim
10. ____ eat good food

B ▶ Listen. Check (✓) the things that Trisha and Ed are going to do on their vacations.

1. ____ hike
2. ____ look at the stars
3. ____ go to a museum
4. ____ bike
5. ____ ski

6. ____ shop
7. ____ get massages
8. ____ ride horses
9. ____ swim
10. ____ eat good food

C ▶ Listen again. Write the checked items from Activity B in the correct place in the Venn diagram to compare and contrast the two hotels. What can you do at each place? What can you do at both places?

Mountain View Lodge   Both   Galaxy Orbit Hotel

D ▶ Pair work.

1. Circle the activities that you like to do. Then rank the eight from 1 (what you like the most) to 8 (what you like the least).

____ camp   ____ see movies   ____ sleep late   ____ ski
____ sunbathe   ____ take tours   ____ take walks   ____ rid

2. What do you like to do on your vacation? Tell your partner six things. Then make a comparing the things you and your partner like to do. Describe the similarities to t

90 Unit 10 Space Tourism

▶ **PREDICTION** activities encourage students to anticipate content in the listenings and readings.

▶ **A VARIETY OF LISTENING COMPREHENSION ACTIVITIES** establishes a solid base of listening competency in students.

▶ **CRITICAL LISTENING SKILLS** build students' comprehension ability with more challenging listening experiences. Skills include listening for gist, identifying tone, distinguishing between pros and cons, identifying cause and effect relationships, and sequencing,

▶ **GRAPHIC ORGANIZERS** illustrate the relationships between ideas in reading, listening, and writing.

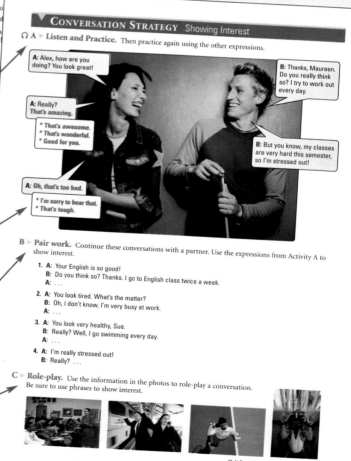

A ▶ Listen and Practice. Then practice again using the other expressions.

A: Alex, how are you doing? You look great!

B: Thanks, Maureen. Do you really think so? I try to work out every day.

A: Really? That's amazing.
* That's awesome.
* That's wonderful.
* Good for you.

B: But you know, my classes are very hard this semester, so I'm stressed out!

A: Oh, that's too bad.
* I'm sorry to hear that.
* That's tough.

B ▶ Pair work. Continue these conversations with a partner. Use the expressions from Activity A to show interest.

1. **A:** Your English is so good!
   B: Do you think so? Thanks. I go to English class twice a week.
   A: . . .

2. **A:** You look tired. What's the matter?
   B: Oh, I don't know. I'm very busy at work.
   A: . . .

3. **A:** You look very healthy, Sue.
   B: Really? Well, I go swimming every day.
   A: . . .

4. **A:** I'm really stressed out!
   B: Really? . . .

C ▶ Role-play. Use the information in the photos to role-play a conversation. Be sure to use phrases to show interest.

▶ **CONVERSATION STRATEGIES** include useful strategies such as showing interest, expressing disbelief, asking for additional information, and asking for and giving opinions.

▶ **CALLOUT BOXES** allow students to substitute additional expressions directly into the conversation model for controlled practice.

▶ **PAIR WORK** uses scaffolded dialogues to bolster students' confidence.

▶ **ROLE-PLAYS** build fluency through interactive, open-ended practice.

xii

- ▶ **STUDY IT** highlights the writing skill in a realistic model.

- ▶ **WRITE IT** implements the writing skill in a step-by-step process.

- ▶ **PREWRITING GRAPHIC ORGANIZERS**, such as mind maps and charts, help students organize their thoughts before writing.

- ▶ **EDITING CHECKS** encourage students to share their writing with classmates for peer review.

WRITING   Using Time Words to Sequence Events

A ▶ Study it.   Read the email. Underline words that show the sequence of events: *first, then, next, after that, finally.*

Hi Laura,

I'm back from Egypt. It was an amazing trip. First, we landed in Cairo. The next day, we went to the Egyptian Museum, and we saw the King Tutankhamun treasures. They were incredible. Then we visited the Pyramids and the Sphinx. We were tired, but the day wasn't over! After that, we flew to Luxor. The next morning, we went to the temple of Karnak. It's huge. Then we took a boat across the river. We visited the Valley of the Kings. The tomb of King Tutankhamun is there. It wasn't very interesting though. All of the treasures are in the museum in Cairo! It was also very hot in the desert, and it was crowded with tourists. Next, we returned to Cairo. The fourth day, we went to the Khan El Khalili market and bought a lot of souvenirs. It was hot and crowded, too, but finally, we relaxed. We went out on a sailboat. It's very quiet out on the Nile. It was a great trip! BTW, do you like the photos? I took them with my new digital camera. I hope you go to Egypt someday.

See you soon!
James

B ▶ Write it.   Write about a trip that you took in the past.

1. Complete these sentences about a past trip. Then add time words to show the sequence.

after that	finally	first	next	then

TIME WORD	ACTION
	I went to
	I saw
	I bought
	I returned home
	I ate
	I visited

...entences from Activity 1 in the correct order.
...ry and discuss it with a classmate.
...e words in your sentences that show the order of events.
...ur story with your classmates. Ask your classmates for more details about their trips.

...ystery

PUTTING IT TOGETHER   Behind the Doors

A ▶ Read.

1. Look at the photo. What is the reading about? Discuss it with your classmates.

The Great Pyramid of Cheops is very large and of course, ancient. The first tourists visited it over two thousand years ago, and it is still the number one tourist site in Egypt today. Archeologists also still study Cheops, but they don't find new things there very often.

In 1992, however, something amazing happened. German archeologists uncovered two tunnels deep inside the pyramid. The tunnels were not on their maps. They were new discoveries! There were two small doors at the end of the tunnels. Scientists built robots and put them into the tunnels. Then, in 2001, a robot made a small hole in one of the doors and

put the camera through the hole. Were there treasures? Was there only dust? No, there was another door!

Archeologists do not agree about what is behind the door. Some think that there is a library of ancient history. Others think there is a treasure, like the treasures found in the tomb of Tutankhamun. Some think there is nothing behind the door. No one knows for sure. For many years, archeologists searched the pyramids, but they didn't find anything. Until 1992, that is.

2. **Checkpoint.**   Write answers to these questions.

1. Where is the Great Pyramid of Cheops? _____
2. What happened there in 1992? _____
3. Where are the doors? _____
4. What do archeologists think is behind the doors? _____

B ▶ Listen.

1. Listen to the conversation and check (✓) the things that Tina and Mike think are behind the door.

	Tina	Mike			Tina	Mike
1. nothing				4. a tomb		
2. gold				5. a mummy		
3. another door				6. bones		

2. **Checkpoint.**   Who do you agree with, Tina or Mike? Why? Discuss this with the class.

C ▶ Wrap it up.

1. [TOEFL® iBT] Tina and Mike's discussion about the Pyramid of Cheops _____
   a. describes things in the pyramid
   b. predicts what is in the pyramid
   c. describes how thieves took the treasures from the pyramid
   d. proves that archeologists know everything about Cheops

2. Write three things that you think are behind the doors. Combine your ideas with a partner's. Then rank your six ideas from the least likely (1) to most likely (6).

Unit 4   It's a Big Mystery   **37**

- ▶ **THE STRATEGIC PAIRING OF READING AND LISTENING IN PUTTING IT TOGETHER** requires students analyze or synthesize information. This builds valuable test-taking skills while recycling critical thinking skills.

- ▶ **CHECKPOINTS** after the reading and the listening ensure comprehension.

- ▶ **WRAP IT UP** provides a non-intimidating TOEFL® iBT style question, which asks students to identify the relationship between the ideas in the reading and those in the listening. It also provides the opportunity for students to discuss and personalize the topic.

1 Tell Me About Yourself

READING AND SPEAKING

A ▶ **Warm up.** Complete the sentences with information about you. Share your answers with a partner.

1. I live in _____.
2. My favorite foods are _____ and _____.
3. I like _____ music.
4. I don't like _____ music.
5. I like _____ and _____.
6. I dislike _____.

Skill Focus — Scanning for Specific Information

To scan, move your eyes quickly across the text until you find the information you need. Don't read every word.

B ▶ **Read.** Scan the articles. Check (✓) the topics that you find.

____ art ____ movies ____ pets

____ children ____ music ____ school

____ interests ____ paparazzi ____ sports

Keira Knightley

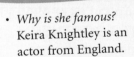

- *Why is she famous?* Keira Knightley is an actor from England.
- *Where does she live?*
5   She lives in London and Los Angeles.
- *What are her **interests**?* Knightley has many interests. She plays the flute, and she loves swimming and soccer.
10 - *What's her **favorite kind of music**?* Knightley loves rock music and hip hop music.
- *What are her **favorite foods**?* Her favorite foods are French fries and ice cream.
- *Does she have a pet?* Yes, she does. She has a cat
15   called Finn.
- *What's her favorite drink?* She likes tea.
- *What's her **favorite kind of movie**?* Knightley loves action movies. She doesn't like her own movies.
- *What does she dislike?* She dislikes paparazzi. She
20   hates the gym. She also doesn't like parties.

Rubens Barrichello

- *Where is he from?* Rubens Barrichello is from Sao Paulo, Brazil. He lives in Monaco, in
25   Europe.
- *What does he do?* Barrichello is a Formula 1 race car driver.
- *What does he do in his free time?* When he is not busy, Barrichello goes to movies with his wife.
30   They like action movies. He also loves sports. He likes golf, running, and tennis.
- *Does he have a nickname?* Yes. His nickname is Rubinho.
- *What's his favorite kind of music?* He likes rock
35   music and Brazilian pop.
- *What's his favorite kind of food?* Barrichello's favorite kind of food is Italian food. He loves spaghetti.
- *What's his favorite drink?*
40   His favorite drink is soda.
- *What does he dislike?* He dislikes paparazzi.

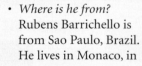

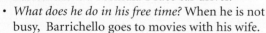

C ▶ **Read again.** Check (✓) True or False for each detail about Knightley and Barrichello.

		True	False
1.	Keira Knightley and Rubens Barrichello are from Monaco.	☐	☐
2.	She loves her own movies.	☐	☐
3.	Barrichello has a nickname.	☐	☐
4.	Knightley's favorite food is spaghetti.	☐	☐
5.	Barrichello and Knightley dislike rock music.	☐	☐
6.	They dislike paparazzi.	☐	☐

D ▶ **Discuss.** Ask and answer the questions with your classmates.

Example:

A: Do you like <u>action</u> movies?
B: Yes, I do.
A: What other kind of movies do you like?
B: I like <u>horror</u> <u>movies</u> and <u>comedies</u>.

A: Do you like <u>pop</u> music?
B: No, I don't.
A: What kind of music do you like?
B: I like <u>jazz</u> and <u>rock</u>.

> **TIP** ▶ **Useful Language**
>
> | **Movies** | **Music** |
> |---|---|
> | action movies | classical |
> | comedies | hip hop |
> | horror movies | jazz |
> | romantic movies | pop |
> | | rap |
> | | rock |

▼ VOCABULARY Categories

A ▶ **Identify.** Complete the chart with information about Knightley, Barrichello, and you.

Category	Keira Knightley	Rubens Barrichello	You
Favorite foods			
Interests		sports: golf, running, tennis	
Favorite kind of movie			
Favorite kind of music			

B ▶ **Pair work.** Ask and answer questions with a partner. Use vocabulary from the chart in Activity A.

Examples:

A: What are your favorite foods?

A: I like Italian food.

B: Hmm. I like sushi and Chinese food. How about you?

The Simple Present: Questions and Answers

We use the simple present to talk about facts (things that are always true), habits, and routines. We use *am*, *is*, and *are* for the verb *be*.

I **eat** a lot of tofu because I **am** a vegetarian.
He **is** a great tennis player. He **practices** every afternoon.
They **are** big movie fans. They **go** to movies on Saturdays.

We use *am*, *are*, *is*, *do*, and *does* in questions that need a *yes* or *no* answer.

Are you a soccer player?	→	**Yes**, I am.
Is she an actor?	→	**Yes**, she is.
Do you like action movies?	→	**No**, I don't. I like comedies.
Does Laura like jazz?	→	**Yes**, she does.

We use *Wh-* questions when we want specific information.

What do you do?	→	I'm a student.
Where is she from?	→	She's from England.
Who is that?	→	That's Rubens Barrichello.
Why are they famous?	→	She's an actor. He's a race car driver.
When do you play tennis?	→	I play on the weekends.
How old are you?	→	Sorry, that's personal information.

A ▶ Practice. Complete the conversations. Then practice with a partner.

1. **A:** _____ are Gael García Bernal and Diego Luna from?

   B: They _____ from Mexico.

2. **A:** _____ is David Beckham so famous?

   B: He _____ a great soccer player from England.

3. **A:** _____ is Steve Jobs?

   B: Oh, he _____ a famous American businessman. You know, Apple computers?

4. **A:** _____ does Gwen Stefani do? _____ she an actor?

   B: No, she _____. She _____ a singer from the United States.

∩ B ▶ Listen. Complete the chart.

Category	Victoria Beckham	David Beckham
Nickname	Her nickname is Posh _____.	His nickname _____.
Occupation	She _____ a singer.	He _____ a _____.
Where from	She _____ from _____.	He _____ from _____.
Lives	She _____ in _____ and _____.	He _____ in _____ and _____.
Likes	She _____.	He _____.

A ▶ Read.

1. Read the article. Underline the names of people.

Bob Geldof is a rock singer, songwriter, TV producer, and human rights activist. He also helps poor people. He lives in England with his family. His three daughters are famous, too. They are not actors, rock
5   singers, or human rights activists. They are famous because they have a famous father. Also, they have interesting names. Fifi Trixibelle is Geldof's first daughter. Fifi is her aunt's name. *Trixie* means "playful", and *Belle* means "beautiful". Fifi has two sisters. One is named Peaches. Peaches are
10   Geldof's favorite fruit. Fifi's other sister is Pixie. *Pixie* means "small and cute". These three names are very unusual.

2. Pair work. Put the words in order to make questions. Ask a partner the questions.

Example: what / Geldof's / favorite fruit / is _What is Geldof's favorite fruit? (Peaches are his favorite fruit.)_

1. is / Geldof / TV producer / a _____

2. why / Bob Geldof / famous / is _____

3. what / mean / *Pixie* / does _____

4. where / live / do / Geldof's daughters _____

5. are / actresses / Geldof's daughters _____

B ▶ Interview. Write five questions using *who, what, when, where, why, are you,* or *do you.* Then interview two classmates.

Questions	Student 1	Student 2
What's your favorite name?	Alison	Joey
Do you have brothers or sisters?	Yes, 2 sisters.	No.
1.		
2.		
3.		
4.		
5.		

A ▶ Discuss. Look at Jacqueline's things. Make a list about her. Discuss it with a partner.

Example: Her nickname is Jacqui.

_____

_____

_____

_____

_____

_____

⌒ B ▶ Listen. Where are Tom and Jacqueline? Circle a, b, c, or d.

a. at work
b. in class
c. at the gym
d. at the movies

⌒ C ▶ Listen again. Check (✓) the things that Jacqueline and Tom talk about.

1. ☐ names
2. ☐ pets
3. ☐ hometowns
4. ☐ occupations

5. ☐ the teacher
6. ☐ interests
7. ☐ movies
8. ☐ tennis

D ▶ Pair work.

1. Complete the card with information that is true for you.

First Name:_____ Last Name:_____ Nickname:_____
Occupation/Part-time Job:_____
Hometown:_____ Interests:_____

2. Get to know your partner better. Complete the card with information that is true for your partner.

Example: A: Do you have a nickname?
B: No, I don't. How about you, Alex?
A: Actually, I do. My friends call me Speedy.

First Name:_____ Last Name:_____ Nickname:_____
Occupation/Part-time Job:_____
Hometown:_____ Interests:_____

A ▶ Listen and practice. Then practice again using the other expressions.

A: What's your name?

A: Sorry, **can you say your last name again?**

* **I didn't catch your name.**
* **I didn't get your name.**

A: Vander . . . . I'm sorry, **can you say that again?**

* **Could you repeat that, please?**
* **I didn't catch that.**

A: Vanderford. Got it.

B: Hi, I'm Maria Vanderford. I'm on the guest list.

B: It's Vanderford.

B: Van-der-ford.

B ▶ Pair work. Continue these conversations with a partner. Use the expressions from Activity A to ask for clarification.

1. **A:** Hi, I'm George Williams. I'm a new student here.
   B: Hi George. I'm Kim Garvey.
   A: Kim, I'm sorry, I . . .

2. **A:** Is Alex there, please?
   B: Sorry, Alex is at work now. His work number is 555-4376.
   A: Sorry, could you . . .

3. **A:** What do you do?
   B: I'm a designer for a company called West Side Design.
   A: I'm sorry, I . . .

4. **A:** When is your birthday?
   B: My birthday? It's March 30th.
   A: . . .

C ▶ Role-play. Use the information to role-play a conversation between Makiko and Edward. Be sure to ask for clarification in your conversation.

Example: **A:** Hello. My name is Makiko.
B: Hi, I'm Edward. I'm sorry, I didn't catch your name.

Name: Makiko Matsuda
Nickname: Ma-chan
Company: Surfing Clothes
Kobe, Japan
Birthday: February 4

Name: Edward Nicholson
Nickname: Nickel
Company: West Side Design
New York, USA
Birthday: July 19

A ▶ Study it. Read the email from Linda.

1. Underline what Linda likes and dislikes.

2. Circle the questions that she asks.

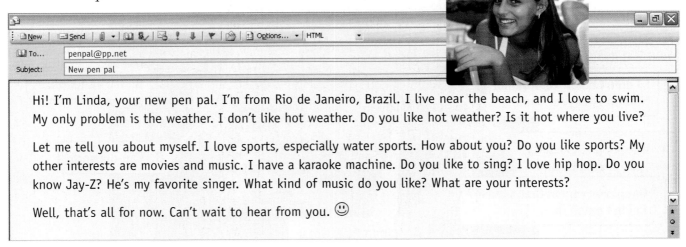

To... penpal@pp.net

Subject: New pen pal

Hi! I'm Linda, your new pen pal. I'm from Rio de Janeiro, Brazil. I live near the beach, and I love to swim. My only problem is the weather. I don't like hot weather. Do you like hot weather? Is it hot where you live?

Let me tell you about myself. I love sports, especially water sports. How about you? Do you like sports? My other interests are movies and music. I have a karaoke machine. Do you like to sing? I love hip hop. Do you know Jay-Z? He's my favorite singer. What kind of music do you like? What are your interests?

Well, that's all for now. Can't wait to hear from you. ☺

B ▶ Write it. Write back to Linda. Complete the email.

1. Write a question for each category. Use *who, what, when, where, how, do you,* or *are you*. Then write the answer with information about you.

Category	Question	Statement
1. Your home	Where do you live?	I live in Seoul, Korea.
2. Weather		
3. Favorite food		
4. Your topic		

2. Complete the email to Linda. You can use information from the chart above.

Hi Linda! Thanks for your email. You live in Rio? How exciting! I live in _____.
I _____ the weather here. It's _____. I like _____ weather.

Yes, I like sports! My favorite sports are _____ and _____. I like _____ music. _____ is my favorite singer. I have two questions for you.
1) What's your _____ food? I love _____ and _____.
2) _____?

I hope to hear from you soon!

3. Compare your email with a partner.
- Circle the things that you have in common.
- Then ask your partner the two questions from your email.

A ▶ Read. Scan the article. Circle the things that Marco spends money on.

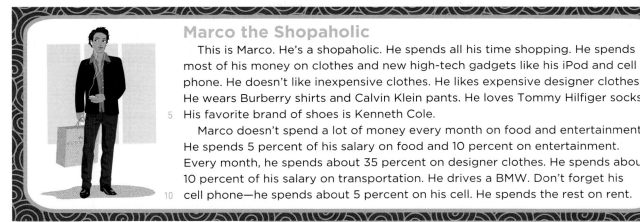

Marco the Shopaholic

This is Marco. He's a shopaholic. He spends all his time shopping. He spends most of his money on clothes and new high-tech gadgets like his iPod and cell phone. He doesn't like inexpensive clothes. He likes expensive designer clothes. He wears Burberry shirts and Calvin Klein pants. He loves Tommy Hilfiger socks.
5 His favorite brand of shoes is Kenneth Cole.

Marco doesn't spend a lot of money every month on food and entertainment. He spends 5 percent of his salary on food and 10 percent on entertainment. Every month, he spends about 35 percent on designer clothes. He spends about 10 percent of his salary on transportation. He drives a BMW. Don't forget his
10 cell phone—he spends about 5 percent on his cell. He spends the rest on rent.

2. Checkpoint. Complete the sentences. Circle a or b.

1. Marco spends a lot of money on _____ .
   a. food   b. high-tech gadgets

2. Marco doesn't like _____ .
   a. inexpensive clothes   b. shopping

B ▶ Listen.

How much does Sharon spend? Write each category in the correct place in the pie chart.

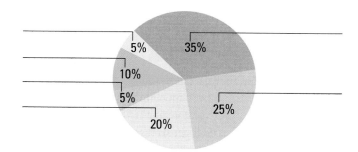

a. transportation
b. cell phone
c. clothes
d. entertainment
e. food
f. rent

C ▶ Wrap it up.

1. (TOEFL® iBT) Compare Marco and Sharon's spending. Complete the chart.

   Example: Sharon spends more on food.

Category	Marco	Sharon
1. Food	5%	35%
2.		
3.		

Category	Marco	Sharon
4.		
5.		
6.		

2. Are you like Marco or Sharon? Discuss with your classmates.

READING AND SPEAKING

A ▶ Warm up. Do you have a healthy lifestyle? Read the statements and check (✓) True or False.

		True	False
1.	I get a lot of exercise.	☐	☐
2.	I get eight hours of sleep a night.	☐	☐
3.	I smoke.	☐	☐
4.	I get stressed out a lot.	☐	☐
5.	I eat healthy food every day.	☐	☐

> **Skill Focus**
> **Skimming for the Main Idea**
> Skimming is reading quickly to identify the topic and the main idea.
> • Look at the title, photos, and diagrams.
> • Read quickly. Don't read every word.
> • Read the first and last two lines of each paragraph.

🎧 **B ▶ Read.** Skim the article to find the main idea. Circle a, b, c, or d.

  a. Japan is an interesting country.
  ⓑ Japanese people live long lives.
  c. Dr. Shibahara is a wonderful doctor.
  d. Older Japanese people are happy.

A Long and Healthy Life

Do you want to live to be 100 years old? You can learn from the Japanese. There are more than 20,000 men and women over 100 years old in Japan. You may ask, "Why do they live so long? They have a lot of stress." Yes, Japanese people often **get stressed out**. They usually
5 work long hours and commute in crowded trains. Just like in other countries, many people have bad habits – they drink alcohol and they smoke. They rarely **take vitamins**. Also, many people don't **get a lot of sleep**, and they hardly ever **take vacations**. So, what is the secret?
  Dr. Shibahara is 92 and has some ideas. He says, "It's the diet. The
10 Japanese diet is very healthy." People drink green tea two or three times a day. They usually eat low-fat meals. They eat fish two or three times a week and occasionally eat meat.
  "Exercise is very important," says Dr. Shibahara. Japanese people usually walk a lot. Dr. Shibahara is very active. He **gets exercise** every
15 day. He always takes the stairs, not the elevator. Dr. Shibahara also spends time with other people. He **takes night classes**. He **goes to the movies** with his grandchildren, and he often **goes on picnics** with his wife. She is 89! Older people in Japan usually live with their children. "Lonely people die young," Dr. Shibahara says. "Eat well, get a lot of
20 exercise, and spend time with family and friends," he advises.

C ▶ Read again. Scan the reading to answer these questions about details.

1. How old is Dr. Shibahara? _____

2. How many people are over 100 years old in Japan? _____

3. Why is life in Japan sometimes stressful? _____

4. What bad habits do some people in Japan have? _____

5. How many times a day do people in Japan usually drink green tea? _____

6. Who do older people in Japan usually live with? _____

D ▶ Pair work. Write your answer to these questions. Then discuss them with a partner.

1. What are your bad habits? What are your good habits?

_____

2. What kind of food do you eat? Is it healthy or unhealthy?

_____

3. Do you want to live to be 100 years old? Explain why or why not.

_____

▼ VOCABULARY Phrases with *get, take,* and *go*

A ▶ Identify. Write these words from the reading in the correct place in the chart.

a lot of sleep	exercise	on a picnic	to the movies
a vacation	night classes	stressed out	vitamins

Verb	Noun or Phrase
	stressed out
get...	
take...	
go...	

B ▶ Pair work. Complete these questions with *get, take,* or *go*. Then ask your partner the questions.

1. Do you _____ stressed out? What stresses you out?

2. When you _____ a vacation or a day off, what do you usually do?

3. What kind of food do people eat when they _____ on a picnic?

4. Why do you _____ English classes?

Adverbs of Frequency and Time Expressions

We use adverbs of frequency for general statements about how often something happens.

Do you ever walk up the stairs? →	I **always** walk up the stairs.	100%
Does she ever commute to work? →	She **usually** commutes to work.	
Do they eat meat? →	Yes. They **often** eat meat.	
Does he get stressed out? →	No. He **sometimes** gets stressed out.	
Do they take vitamins? →	They **rarely** take vitamins.	
How often do you take the elevator? →	I **never** take the elevator.	0%

We use time expressions to be more specific about how often something happens.

How often does he go to work? →	He goes to work **every day.**
Do they like tea? →	Yes, they drink green tea **once or twice a day.**
How often do you take a vacation? →	I take a vacation **once a year.**
Do the Japanese work a lot? →	Yes, they go to work **five days a week.**

A ▶ Practice. Complete conversations 1–3 with an adverb of frequency from the box. Complete conversations 4–6 with a time expression from the box.

1. **A:** Do you ever feel stress?

   B: Yes, I _____ get stressed out! I have a difficult job.

2. **A:** Do you drink tea?

   B: I _____ drink tea, but I usually drink coffee.

3. **A:** Do you like hamburgers?

   B: Actually, I'm a vegetarian. I _____ eat hamburgers.

4. **A:** How often does she exercise?

   B: She goes to the gym _____. She usually goes on Saturday or Sunday.

5. **A:** Does he have a healthy diet?

   B: Yes, he does, and he takes vitamins _____.

6. **A:** You work hard. When do you relax?

   B: Well, I take an art class _____, on Tuesday and Thursday.

> **TIP** ▶
> **Adverbs of Frequency**
> • never
> • sometimes
> • often
> **Time Expressions**
> • once a week
> • twice a week
> • every day

B ▶ Pair work. Ask and answer questions about Rosa's weekly schedule.

Example: A: How often does Rosa go to the gym? → **B:** She goes to the gym every day.

Sunday	Monday	Tuesday	Wednesday	Thursday	Friday	Saturday
• gym	• gym	• gym	• gym	• gym	• gym	• gym
• 2:00 play soccer	• work	• work	• work	• work	• work	
	• 6:30 dinner with friends	• 7:00–9:30 English class		• 7:00–9:30 English class		• 7:30 dinner with friends

A ▶ Listen.

1. How often does Dave do the following things? Write a, b, c, or d on each line.

    1. _____ drink soda   a. rarely

    2. _____ exercise   b. never

    3. _____ overeat   c. every day

    4. _____ get eight hours of sleep   d. usually

2. Pair work. Ask your partner about the actions in the chart and add one of your own. Do your partner and Dave have the same lifestyle?

    Example: **A:** How often do you get eight hours of sleep?
                 B: I always get eight hours of sleep!
                 You write: *My partner always gets eight hours of sleep.*

ACTION	ABOUT YOUR PARTNER
1. GET EIGHT HOURS OF SLEEP	
2. EXERCISE	
3. DRINK SODA	
4. OVEREAT	
5. *YOUR IDEA:*	

B ▶ Interview. Ask five classmates about their habits. Are they healthy? Write each person's name under 1 to 5 in the chart.

    Example: **Lee:**   Are you a healthy person?

              Maya: Oh, I think so. I exercise six times a week. I always eat healthy food. I never eat sugar. How about you?

              Lee: Well, I love to watch TV. I rarely exercise. I'm definitely a couch potato. I think you're a health nut.

Couch Potato					Health Nut
1	2	3	4	5	
Lee				Maya	

A ▶ **Discuss.** Look at the three students' lockers. Which things do you have? Circle them.

1.    **2.**    **3.**

🎧 **B** ▶ **Listen.** Paul is talking with his doctor. Read the statements. Check (✓) True or False.

	True	False
1. Paul is a student.	☐	☐
2. Paul plays tennis once or twice a week.	☐	☐
3. Paul eats junk food every day.	☐	☐
4. Paul never takes vitamins.	☐	☐
5. Paul usually smokes.	☐	☐
6. Paul often practices the guitar.	☐	☐

🎧 **C** ▶ **Listen again.** Look at the pictures in Activity A. Which locker is Paul's?

D ▶ **Pair work.** Work with your partner to identify items and make inferences.

Skill Focus **Making Inferences**
When we make inferences, we read or listen to information and make guesses about additional information that is not stated directly.

1. Look at the picture. Which things do you have in your wallet or bag? Check (✓) them.

___ receipt   ___ keys   ___ paperback book

___ school ID   ___ cell phone   ___ pen

___ library card   ___ gym membership card   ___ candy

2. Put five things from your bag or your wallet on the desk. Then ask and answer questions about your partner's routines and habits.

Example: **A**: I see two Starbucks receipts! How often do you go to Starbucks?

          B: I go twice a day!

TIP ▶ **Useful Language**
• How many books do you read every week?
• How often do you use your cell phone?

⌒ **A** ▶ **Listen and Practice.** Then practice again using the other expressions.

A: Alex, how are you doing? You look great!

A: Really? That's amazing.
* That's awesome.
* That's wonderful.
* Good for you.

A: Oh, that's too bad.
* I'm sorry to hear that.
* That's tough.

B: Thanks, Maureen. Do you really think so? I try to work out every day.

B: But you know, my classes are very hard this semester, so I'm stressed out!

B ▶ **Pair work.** Continue these conversations with a partner. Use the expressions from Activity A to show interest.

1. **A:** Your English is so good!
   B: Do you think so? Thanks. I go to English class twice a week.
   A: . . .

2. **A:** You look tired. What's the matter?
   B: Oh, I don't know. I'm very busy at work.
   A: . . .

3. **A:** You look very healthy, Sue.
   B: Really? Well, I go swimming every day.
   A: . . .

4. **A:** I'm really stressed out!
   B: Really? . . .

C ▶ **Role-play.** Use the information in the photos to role-play a conversation. Be sure to use phrases to show interest.

A ▶ Study it. Underline the topic sentence in each paragraph. The topic sentence tells the main idea of the paragraph.

Soo Young Kim

Soo Young Kim has a very busy life. She has classes at the university every day. One of her classes is English. Her English class meets twice a week. She
5 has a part-time job. She works in a supermarket. She also likes volunteering. On Saturday mornings, she visits older people in her neighborhood. She talks to them, and
10 goes for walks with them.

In her free time, Soo Young has fun. Music is important to her. She plays the piano. On Friday nights, Soo Young often goes to karaoke with her friends. Sports are a big part of her life. She is a very good volleyball player. She likes watching sports on TV, too.

B ▶ Write it. Learn to identify and write a topic sentence.

1. Complete each paragraph with the best topic sentence. Circle a, b, or c.

 1. _____. The beaches are wonderful. The weather is amazing and the food is great, too. I love the blue sky and the beautiful white sand. The city also has some very interesting old buildings.

    a. I love Miami, Florida.　　b. The ocean is warm.　　c. I love swimming.

 2. Let me tell you about my part-time job. _____. It's a vegetarian restaurant. We are busy every day. It's a difficult job, but the food is great. We have some really nice customers. However, some customers are rude. They really stress me out!

    a. I love food.　　b. It's downtown.　　c. I work at a Korean restaurant.

 3. _____. She is from Mexico, but now she lives in Los Angeles. Her first name means peace. She loves basketball and she is a big fan of the LA Lakers NBA team. She also loves salsa dancing. Donna Karan is her favorite designer.

    a. I think Salma Hayek is beautiful.　b. Salma Hayek is a famous actor.　c. I want to be an actor.

2. Write a topic sentence for the following paragraph.

_____.

I go two or three times a week. I watch movies at home, too. I often rent DVDs. I don't have a favorite movie, but I do have a favorite actor. I love George Clooney. I think he is very talented and good-looking.

3. Read your partner's topic sentence. Does the topic sentence tell the main idea of the paragraph?

A ▶ Read.

1. Choose the best title. Circle a, b, or c.

    a. How to Get Enough Sleep   b. How to Relieve Stress   c. How to Live a Long Life

> Doctors say that people don't get enough sleep. The average person needs about eight hours of sleep a night. However, most people only get about six and a half hours of sleep every night. This is because bad habits and stress often disrupt sleep
> 5 patterns. Often, people watch TV in bed and eat late at night. As a result, they can't sleep. For other people, stress is a real problem. Exercise, relaxing activities, and good food help reduce stress and help you sleep.

To be healthy, you need to get enough sleep. Here is some more advice.

Do	Don't
Go to bed early every night.	Don't eat after 8:00 p.m.
Exercise three times a week.	Don't drink after 8:00 p.m.
Eat healthy, low-fat meals.	Don't work or study late.
Get lots of fresh air.	Don't work or watch TV in bed.

2. Checkpoint. Write answers to these questions.

    1. How many hours of sleep do people need? _____

    2. Why don't people sleep enough? Give two reasons. _____

    3. What three things help reduce stress? _____

B ▶ Listen.

1. Check (✓) three reasons that Steven is unhappy.

    a. __ He doesn't like his job.   d. __ He is always busy.

    b. __ He doesn't get enough sleep.   e. __ He smokes.

    c. __ He is always tired.   f. __ He overeats.

2. Checkpoint. Check (✓) True or False.

	True	False
1. Steven goes to bed early every night.	☐	☐
2. Steven often exercises.	☐	☐
3. Steven eats in restaurants five or six times a week.	☐	☐
4. Steven leaves the office at 7:00.	☐	☐

C ▶ Wrap it up.

1. **TOEFL® iBT** What advice in the reading is good for Steven?

2. List five things you do when you can't sleep. Discuss them with your classmates.

3 Where Do You Hang Out?

▼ READING AND SPEAKING

A ▶ Warm up. Where do you usually go on the weekend? Check (✓) the places below.

1. __ to a coffee shop
2. __ to the gym
3. __ to an interesting part of town

4. __ to a movie theater
5. __ to my friend's home
6. __ to a museum

∩ **B ▶ Read.** Skim the two articles. Underline the main idea in each.

Zona Rosa is a very exciting part of Mexico City. Zona Rosa means *pink zone*. There are many **pink buildings** in the area.
Zona Rosa is popular with young people
5   and tourists. There are some great **bars**, **nightclubs**, and **restaurants**. It's a good place to meet friends on weekends. Saturday nights are really busy and a lot of fun.
The area is also famous for **antique stores**,
10 but there aren't any bargains. It's quite expensive. When you get tired of shopping, there are some interesting places to see. There are some famous **fountains**, **statues**, and churches in the area.

15 **Central Park** is a wonderful place in the middle of Manhattan. There are many **trees**, lakes, and places to play baseball or soccer. There are also tennis courts and jogging paths. There is also a small zoo and a **boathouse**. In addition,
20 Central Park has some interesting statues, fountains, and **exhibitions**. Be sure to visit Strawberry Fields, the John Lennon Memorial. New Yorkers and visitors like Central Park because there are some good bars and restaurants, and there is always
25 a lot to do. Also, there isn't any traffic, and it's usually peaceful and quiet. This is very unusual for New York!

C ▶ Read again. Compare Zona Rosa and
Central Park. Use the words from the
box to complete the Venn diagram.

| antique stores | bars | fountains | pink buildings | statues |
| exhibitions | boathouse | nightclubs | restaurants | trees |

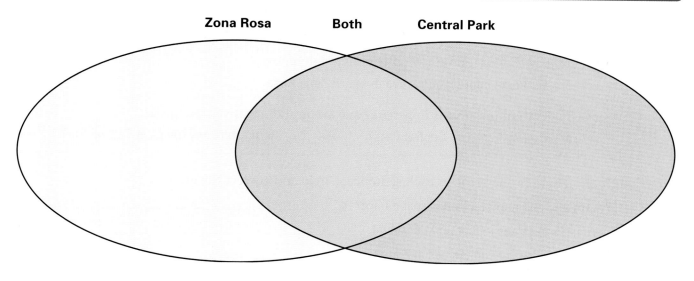

Zona Rosa   **Both**   **Central Park**

D ▶ Pair work. Ask and answer these questions with a partner.

1. Do you prefer quiet places like parks or busy places like Zona Rosa?
2. How often do you hang out with your friends? Where do you go?

▼ VOCABULARY Public Places

A ▶ Identify. Complete the chart with words from the box. Some words can go in more than one
category. You can also add words from the reading and your own ideas.

amusement park	gym
bank	mall
café	park
campus	restaurant
club	subway station
doctor's office	theater

PLACES THAT PEOPLE GO FOR _____	PLACE
ENTERTAINMENT	
BUSINESS OR SHOPPING	
HEALTH REASONS	
OTHER REASONS	

B ▶ Pair work. Which places from Activity A do you visit frequently in your city or town? Tell your
partner. Does your partner know these places?

Example: A: I go to Mocha House once or twice a week. Do you know it?
B: Mocha House? No, I don't know it.
C: It's a café on Main Street.

There is / There are with *some* and *any*

In statements, we use *there is* with singular nouns and *there are* with plural nouns.

> **There is** a small zoo in the park.
> **There are** a lot of great restaurants in that neighborhood.

In questions, we use *Is there* with singular nouns and *Are there* with plural nouns.

> **Is there** a good coffee shop in the area? → Yes, there is.
> **Are there** many trees in Central Park? → Yes, there are.

We use *some* with plural nouns in affirmative statements.

> There are **some** interesting places to see in Zona Rosa.

We use *any* with plural nouns in general questions and negative statements.

> Are there **any** banks in Central Park? → No, there aren't **any** banks in Central Park.

A ▶ Practice. There is one error in each sentence. Circle and correct the error.

1. Is there any cheap restaurants around here? _____

2. There isn't any trees in that neighborhood. _____

3. There are any really cool places in Zona Rosa. _____

4. There aren't some really delicious things on the menu. _____

5. Are there a post office near here? _____

6. There's any bank on Main Street. _____

🎧 **B ▶ Listen.** Check (✓) True or False about Dae Hak Ro, a popular area in Seoul, Korea.

	True	False
1. There aren't any good restaurants in Dae Hak Ro.	☐	☐
2. There's a subway stop in the area.	☐	☐
3. Sorak-san is a bar in the area.	☐	☐
4. There aren't any museums in the area.	☐	☐

A ▶ **Read.**

1. Underline foods and drinks in the article.

ChikaLicious

Lidia Vasquez is from Mexico, but she lives in New York. She loves New York, especially the variety of restaurants. Her favorite restaurant is called ChikaLicious. There aren't many restaurants like ChikaLicious. It only serves dessert,
5 cheese, and drinks. In fact, there aren't any other foods on the menu. There aren't even many drinks on the menu, only coffee, tea, and wine. "I spend hours at ChikaLicious," Lidia says. "I usually have some coffee, some cheese, and a piece of cake. I know cheese and coffee are strange together. But
10 really, it's delicious. The restaurant is relaxing, too. There are always fresh flowers on the tables, and there are lots of friendly people."

2. Pair work. Ask and answer the questions below. Use *there is*, *there isn't*, *there are*, or *there aren't* in your answers.

> **Example: A:** Are there many different kinds of food at ChikaLicious?
> **B:** No, there aren't many kinds of food at ChikaLicious.

1. What's on the menu at ChikaLicious?
2. Why is the ChikaLicious menu unusual?
3. Why does Lidia like this restaurant?
4. Is there anything on the menu that you like or don't like?

B ▶ **Group work.** Complete the chart with information about you. Then discuss it with your classmates.

> **Example: A:** My favorite place is Disneyland.
> **B:** Why do you like it?
> **A:** Well, there are a lot of interesting things to do.
> **B:** Are there any bars and restaurants?
> **A:** Well, there are some nice restaurants. There aren't any bars.

My favorite part of town:	My favorite restaurant:	My favorite place: Disneyland
Why I like it:	Why I like it:	Why I like it: There are a lot of interesting things to do.

A ▸ Discuss. Predict, or guess, where the people below want to go. Write a, b, c, or d on each line.

a. the gym   b. a jazz club   c. a coffee shop   d. a park

1. Jenn ____    2. Kevin ____

3. Alan ____    4. Karen ____

B ▸ Listen. Confirm your predictions from Activity A. Listen and check your answers.

C ▸ Listen again. Make an inference and match the names with the information about the people.

1. ___ Alan   a. likes jazz
2. ___ Jenn   b. needs to relax
3. ___ Kevin   c. doesn't feel healthy
4. ___ Karen   d. likes outdoor sports

D ▸ Pair work.

1. What is your opinion of the places Alan, Jenn, Kevin, and Karen discussed? Discuss with your partner.

coffee shop	gym	jazz club	park

> **Example: A:** I don't like gyms. I like to exercise outside. I usually go to the park and exercise.
> **B:** Really? I go to the gym about three times a week. I love it!

2. Tell your classmates about your partner.

> **Example:** My partner doesn't like gyms. He likes to exercise outside. He likes parks.

∩ **A** ▶ **Listen and practice.** Then practice again using the other expressions.

A: Where do you like to hang out?

A: Why's that?

* **How come?**
* **Can you explain why?**

A: Oh, really? **Tell me more.**

* **Tell me why?**
* **Go on.**

B: I like clubs, department stores . . . you know, busy places.

B: Well, I like meeting new people.

B: I just think people are interesting.

B ▶ **Pair work.** Continue these conversations with a partner. Use the expressions from Activity A to ask for additional information.

1. **A:** What's your major?
   B: English.
   A: Wow. That sounds difficult.
   B: Actually, I love it.
   A: . . .

2. **A:** What do you like to do on weekends?
   B: Well, usually, I take judo classes.
   A: . . .

3. **A:** What's your favorite part of town?
   B: Hmm. I really like Central Square.
   A: . . .

4. **A:** How often do you go to the mall?
   B: To the mall? Never!
   A: . . .

C ▶ **Group work.** Discuss one thing that you dislike. Be sure to ask your classmates for additional information.

Example: A: I really dislike amusement parks.
   B: Really? Why's that?
   A: Because they're too crowded and loud.
       And I don't like rides—they make me feel sick.

> **TIP** ▶ **Useful Language**
>
> * I can't stand it / them.
> * I think it's / they're boring.

A ▶ Study it. Circle the connecting words *and*, *but*, and *or*, and underline the ideas that each connecting word links.

There is a famous building in New York City with a confusing name. Its name is Madison Square Garden, but it is not a garden. Many people visit it each year. There is boxing, basketball, or ice hockey all year round. There are over 20,000 seats and over
5   100 luxury boxes in the main arena. Madison Square Garden is exciting, but it's expensive. A good seat can cost US $500! It is also a popular place for concerts and business meetings. Almost every day, there is a convention in the main arena or in the theater. When you go to New York, be sure to see Madison Square Garden.

B ▶ Write it. Write about a landmark in your city.

1. Complete the chart with details or facts about a landmark in your city.

DETAIL	CONNECTING WORD / FUNCTION	DETAIL
1.	*AND* (ADD INFORMATION)	
2.	*BUT* (OPPOSITE IDEA)	
3.	*OR* (ANOTHER CHOICE)	

2. Write three sentences to combine the details in your chart. Then add one more sentence.

    Example: The National Palace Museum is an attractive building, and there's a lot to see inside. It's really big, but there is a very good guided tour.

> **TIP ▶** The **conjunctions**, or **connecting words** *and*, *but*, and *or*, connect words, phrases, and clauses. If they connect two independent clauses, then we put a comma before the conjunction.
> *Its name is Madison Square Garden,* **but** *it is not a garden.*
> If the first clause is independent, and the second is dependent, then we don't use a comma.
> *It is also a popular place for concerts* **and** *business meetings.*
> If it's a list of words or phrases, we include a comma.
> *You can watch boxing, basketball,* **or** *ice hockey all year round.*

3. Edit your sentences.
- Circle the conjunctions and write what each one does. (Does it add information, show an opposite idea, or give another choice?)
- Underline the details in each sentence.
- Do you use the correct conjunction with your details?

A ▶ Read.

1. Read the paragraphs and the opinions.
Check (✓) the opinion that you agree with.

    1. ☐ Telecommuting sounds great!
    2. ☐ Telecommuting sounds boring and lonely!

2. Checkpoint. Write *R* for Rick and *J* for Jeff in the correct category.

Category	Rick or Jeff?
1. telecommuter	
2. office worker	
3. marketing manager	
4. sales manager	

B ▶ Listen.

1. Check (✓) the correct business card for Linda.

a. _____   b. _____

2. Checkpoint. Answer these questions with a partner.

    1. What kind of company does Linda work for?
    2. Is it a big company or a small company?

C ▶ Wrap it up.

1. [TOEFL® iBT] Circle the two categories that describe Linda.

    1. telecommuter OR office worker
    2. sales manager OR marketing manager

2. List five advantages of telecommuting. List five disadvantages.

Advantages	Disadvantages

Meet Rick. He is a marketing manager. He works in an office in downtown Chicago, but 5 he lives in the suburbs. From Monday to Friday, he gets up early. He puts on a suit and tie and goes to the train station. He 10 spends two hours a day commuting. He reads the newspaper or a book on the train, and he listens to his iPod. Rick enjoys his work. He meets a 15 lot of people every day. Also, he talks with his friends in the office. "I spend a lot of time with my friends. We chat, we go for lunch," he says. What does he think about his job? "I like my job, but I don't like the commute. I spend two 20 hours on the train every day, and my monthly rail pass is really expensive."

Jeff's life is very different from Rick's life. Jeff is a sales manager, but he doesn't travel to work every day. He works in a home office. 25 He's a telecommuter. "I get up at 8:45 every morning and start work at 9:00 a.m.! Sometimes I work in my pajamas," he says.

"I am on the phone with customers all day, 30 and I use my home computer." Jeff likes his job. "I save a lot of money because I don't drive or take the train 35 to work. Also, I have lunch at home. But sometimes I'm a bit lonely. I don't see any friends during the day."

LISTENING AND CONVERSATION Let's join a gym!

A ▶ **Warm up.** Write a phrase from the box under each photo. Then ask and answer questions about the activities with a partner.

> **Example: A:** Do you ever go to the gym?
> **B:** Yes, I sometimes go to the gym.

> drink coffee
> eat junk food
> get eight hours of sleep
> get stressed out
> go to the gym
> walk to work or to school

1. _____

2. _____

3. _____

4. _____

5. _____

6. _____

⌒ **B** ▶ **Listen.** Check (✓) what each person does. Write an ✗ for things the person rarely or never does.

	Kristy	Jim
Gets stressed out		
Walks to work		
Watches a lot of TV		
Eats junk food		
Smokes		

C ▸ Pair work. Discuss these questions with a partner.

   1. Ask a partner questions to check your answers in Activity B.

      Example: A: Does Kristy get stressed out?
           B: _____

   2. Why does Kristy want to join a gym?

   3. Does Jim want to join a gym? Why or why not?

⌒ D ▸ Listen again.

1. Categorize Kristy's and Jim's habits as healthy or unhealthy. Use information from Activity B.

	Healthy Habits	Unhealthy Habits
Kristy		
Jim		

2. Listen and add more information to the chart. Add adverbs of frequency (*always, usually, often, sometimes, rarely, never*) or time expressions (*every day, every night*) for each activity.

3. Do you think Kristy is a very healthy person? Why or why not? Do you think Jim is a very healthy person? Why or why not?

E ▸ Interview. Add a question to the chart. Interview three classmates. Complete the chart.

	NAME:_____	NAME:_____	NAME:_____
1. HOW MANY TIMES A WEEK DO YOU EXERCISE?			
2. HOW MUCH SLEEP DO YOU USUALLY GET?			
3. DO YOU EAT JUNK FOOD? HOW OFTEN?			
4. YOUR QUESTION:			

A ▶ Vocabulary boost! Look at the photos in the travel brochures in Activity B. What do people do at each of these places? At both places? Use words from the box to complete the Venn diagram.

eat at a restaurant	go ice skating	go swimming	play volleyball
get fresh air	go skiing	have a picnic	relax in the sand
get some exercise	go snowboarding	listen to the ocean	sunbathe

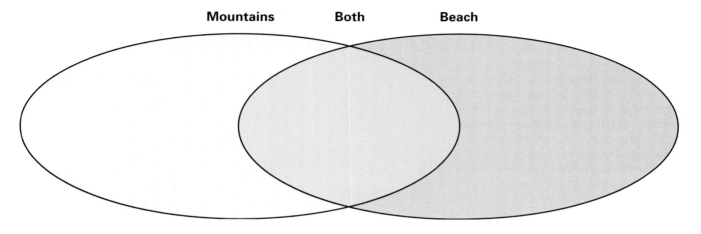

Mountains   **Both**   **Beach**

B ▶ Read. Read the travel brochures. Then underline the main idea in each paragraph.

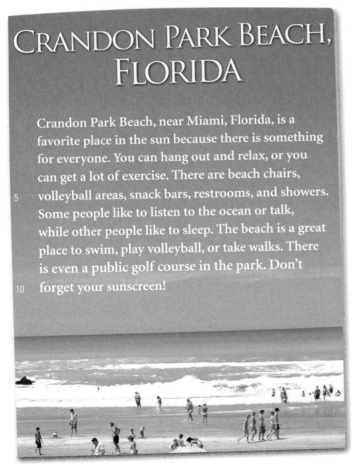

CRANDON PARK BEACH, FLORIDA

Crandon Park Beach, near Miami, Florida, is a favorite place in the sun because there is something for everyone. You can hang out and relax, or you can get a lot of exercise. There are beach chairs,
5 volleyball areas, snack bars, restrooms, and showers. Some people like to listen to the ocean or talk, while other people like to sleep. The beach is a great place to swim, play volleyball, or take walks. There is even a public golf course in the park. Don't
10 forget your sunscreen!

Stowe, Vermont

Do you like to ski or snowboard? For a truly relaxing winter vacation, come to Stowe, Vermont, in the Green Mountains. Enjoy the fresh mountain air and snow at Mount Mansfield. Do you like ice skating?
5 There is a small ice-skating rink near the ski area. At the bottom of the mountain, there are several wonderful restaurants for eating inside or outside. At the hotel next to the ski area, there is a heated pool and a hot tub. In the town of Stowe, there are plenty
10 of antique shops and restaurants. Stowe, Vermont, is a great place for a winter vacation.

C ▸ Discuss. What do you think? Discuss these questions.

1. Which place sounds more interesting to you—the beach at Crandon Park in Florida or the ski area at Stowe, Vermont? Why?
2. On vacation, do you like to relax or do you prefer to exercise?

D ▸ Read again. Answer these questions.

1. In each paragraph, circle the connecting words *and* and *or*.
2. Underline six places or things that you can find at Crandon Park Beach.
3. Write the activities that people enjoy at Crandon Park Beach.

_____

4. What is there in Stowe, Vermont? Underline the places in the paragraph.
5. Write the activities that people do in Stowe.

_____

E ▸ Write about it.

1. Write five questions about vacations.

   1. Where _____?
   2. How often _____?
   3. Are _____?
   4. What _____?
   5. _____?

2. Create a chart like the one on page 27, Activity E. Interview a classmate and complete the chart.

My Interview with _____

3. Tell your classmates three things you learned about your partner.

4 It's a Big Mystery

READING AND SPEAKING

A ▶ Warm up. What do you know about the mysteries in the chart? Do you think they are real? Check (✓) the boxes.

Mystery	I know a lot about these.	I know a little about these.	I don't know anything about these.	I don't think these are real.
1. UFOs and aliens	☐	☐	☐	☐
2. Crop Circles	☐	☐	☐	☐

B ▶ Read. Look at the photos in the article. Predict what the reading is about. Circle a, b, c, or d. Tell your partner.

a. farmers

b. crop circles

c. students

d. UFOs and aliens

One morning in 1977,

a farmer in England discovered a large, **unusual** circle in his cornfield. He was surprised and confused. Newspaper
5 reporters visited the field, and all around the world, scientists discussed the circles. At first, they said that the crops had an unusual disease. Then something very **strange** happened. Other farmers came
10 forward. They had crop circles, too. One night, many scientists stayed up in the fields. They saw **mysterious** lights. The next day, the scientists **discovered** new crop circles. The stories of the circles grew.

15 Eventually, people believed different things about the crop circles. There were tales about aliens, new kinds of lightning, and other mysteries. Then, some university students came forward and showed a TV
20 crew how to make a crop circle. The crop circles were a **hoax**! Finally, people knew the truth. The story of the crop circles wasn't **exciting** anymore, or so people thought. Just a few years ago, a historian found a
25 drawing from 1647. The drawing showed a strange circle in a field, a crop circle. Was this a hoax, too? No one is sure. The story of crop circles continues.

Crop circles

Reporters at work

C ▶ Read again. Sequence these events. Number them from 1 to 6.

    a. ____ Scientists saw lights in the cornfields.

    b. ____ Some people believed that aliens made the circles.

    c. ____ People learned that the mystery was a hoax.

    d. _1_ A farmer discovered a circle in his cornfield.

    e. ____ Scientists said the crops had a strange disease.

    f. ____ University students showed people how to make a crop circle.

> **Skill Focus**   **Sequencing**
> When we sequence events, we put them in order of what happened first, second, third, and so on.

D ▶ Discuss. Ask and answer these questions with your classmates.

    1. In your opinion, who or what made (or makes) the crop circles?

    2. Do you have a favorite mystery? Explain. Do you like mysteries? Why or why not?

    3. Describe the picture. Do you like to play tricks? What do you think of people who play tricks?

VOCABULARY   Using Synonyms

A ▶ Identify. Three words in each line have the same or a similar meaning. Underline them. Put an X through the word that is different.

1. mysterious	unusual	uncomfortable	strange
2. boring	interesting	exciting	fascinating
3. hoax	trick	joke	book
4. discover	come across	tell	find

B ▶ Practice. Write the sentences again using a synonym of the underlined word.

    1. Some people don't believe crop circles are <u>hoaxes</u>.

    _____

    2. Every few years, someone <u>comes across</u> a new crop circle.

    _____

    3. The drawing from 1647 is still <u>fascinating</u> to many historians.

    _____

    4. There are no explanations for many <u>mysterious</u> things like crop circles.

    _____

GETTING INTO GRAMMAR

The Simple Past

Statements

We use the simple past to talk about actions that start and finish in the past.
We add -d or -ed to form the simple past of regular verbs.

    (arrive) Many scientists **arrived.**   (visit) Reporters **visited** the cornfields.

There are many irregular verbs. Here are two. (See page 132 for more irregular verbs.)

    (make) Students **made** the crop circles.   (see) People **saw** them.

We use *didn't* + the base form of the verb to form the negative simple past.

    (make) The farmers **didn't make** the crop circles.

The verb *be* is used differently.

    (be) The farmer **was** surprised. The circles **were** very big. They **were not** easy to hide.

Questions

We use *was* and *were* for yes/no questions with *be*.

    (be) **Was** it a hoax?   →   Yes, it was. / No, it wasn't.
    (be) **Were** they surprised?   →   Yes, they were. / No, they weren't.

We use *did* for yes/no questions with other verbs.

    (go) **Did** you **go** to school yesterday?   →   Yes, I did. / No, I didn't.

We use *did* + subject + the base form of the verb for *Wh*-questions in the past.

    (talk) What **did** the scientists **talk** about?   (see) When **did** people **see** lights in the fields?

A ▶ Practice. Complete the paragraph with verbs in the simple past.

    The story of the *Mary Celeste* is a very famous mystery. On December 4, 1872, sailors on another ship (discover) _____ the *Mary Celeste* in the middle of the ocean. They (signal) _____ to the ship, but the crew of the *Mary Celeste* (respond, no) _____. The
5 sailors (go) _____ aboard the ship, but they (find, no) _____ any passengers or crew. The sailors (look) _____ everywhere, but there (be, no) _____ any people on board. It was a mystery. After some time, people (forget) _____ about the *Mary Celeste*. Then Arthur Conan Doyle, later the author of the Sherlock Holmes novels, (write) _____ a book about it, and people (be) _____ interested again.

B ▶ Pair work. Use the words to ask and answer questions in the present or past.

    Example: you / like / mysteries   <u>Do you like mysteries? (Yes, I think they're exciting.)</u>

    1. the story about the *Mary Celeste* / be / a hoax _____

    2. students / make / the crop circles _____

    3. the *Mary Celeste* and crop circles / be / interesting topics _____

A ▶ Listen and write.

1. Listen to the information about Elvis Presley. Complete each sentence. Circle a, b, or c.

1. Elvis was born in _____.
a. 1935   b. 1930   c. 1925

2. Elvis played _____ in high school.
a. football   b. basketball   c. baseball

3. Elvis worked part-time _____.
a. in a store   b. on a farm   c. for a record producer

4. Elvis graduated from high school in _____.
a. 1953   b. 1954   c. 1955

5. How many number one hit songs did Elvis sing?
a. under 25   b. 25   c. over 25

6. When did Elvis Presley die? _____.
a. in 1977   b. in 1987   c. He didn't die.

Elvis Presley

2. Pair work. Write a question about each item below. Then write the answer with information about Elvis and about yourself. Then ask and answer the questions with a partner.

Question	Elvis	Me	Partner
1. Born:			
2. Sports:			
3. Work:			
4. Graduated from high school:			

B ▶ Group work. Write two true details about your life in the past. Write one false detail. Ask your classmates to guess which details are true and which detail is false.

Example: I had a pet monkey when I was a child.

> **TIP**   **Useful Language**
> - I think that's true.
> - I don't think that's true.
> - I think that's false.

1. _____

2. _____

3. _____

A ▶ Discuss. The pictures tell a story. Predict three things that happen in the story.

A	B	C	D	E

⌂ B ▶ Listen. Sequence the events in the correct order from 1 to 5. Number 1 shows what happened first, and number 5 shows what happened last.

a. ____ The man learned that his briefcase was gone.

b. ____ The taxi driver called the businessman.

c. ____ The man left a briefcase in the taxi.

d. ____ The taxi driver became famous.

e. ____ The taxi driver and the businessman met again at the police station.

⌂ C ▶ Listen again. Check (✓) the correct statement in each pair of statements.

1. ____ a. The man's briefcase was full of jewelry and diamonds.

____ b. The man's briefcase was full of gold coins.

2. ____ a. The man and the taxi driver met at the airport.

____ b. The man called the taxi driver from the airport.

3. ____ a. The value of the things in the briefcase was $20,000.

____ b. The value of the things in the briefcase was $1,000,0000.

4. ____ a. The man felt very foolish.

____ b. The man felt very lucky.

D ▶ Pair work.

1. Make a list of two lucky and two unlucky events in your life.

_____

_____

_____

_____

> **TIP ▶ Useful Language**
>
> - Once, I found . . .
> - Once, I met . . .
> - Once, I forgot . . .
> - Once, I lost . . .
> - Once, I . . .

2. Ask and answer questions about Activity 1 with a partner.

Example: A: Once, I lost my wedding ring.

B: What happened?

A: Well, I went to Italy on vacation and . . .

A ► **Listen and practice.** Then practice again using the other phrases.

A: What happened?

B: Oh, you're not going to believe this. A waiter spilled soup on me.

A: What?
You're kidding.

* **You've got to be joking.**
* **Really?**

B: It's true. And then he dropped my main course on the floor.

A: Dropped your main course? **That's unbelievable!**

* **No way!**
* **I can't believe it!**

B: I know, and it was at my favorite restaurant.

B ► **Pair work.** Continue these conversations with a partner. Use the phrases from Activity A to express disbelief.

1. **A:** You are not going to believe this, but I met Johnny Depp last night.
   B: Johnny Depp? . . .

2. **A:** I went to England, and I saw a crop circle on a farm!
   B: What? . . .

3. **A:** Let's have lunch.
   B: No thanks. I'm not eating today or tomorrow.
   A: . . .

4. **A:** Green hair is very fashionable now!
   B: Green hair? . . .
   A: . . .

C ► **Role-play.** Look at the photos and role-play a conversation. Be sure to use phrases to express disbelief.

My brother loves spiders.

Deepak Gupta of India sang for 54 hours and 42 minutes.

In China, there are 90 cities with over one million people.

A ▶ Study it. Read the email. Underline words that show the sequence of events: *first, then, next, after that, finally.*

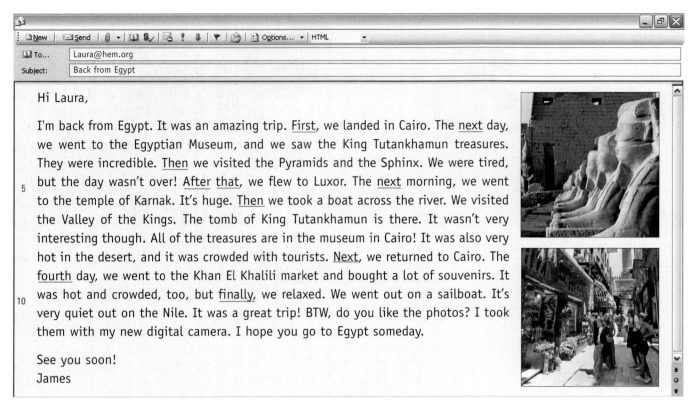

To... Laura@hem.org

Subject: Back from Egypt

Hi Laura,

I'm back from Egypt. It was an amazing trip. First, we landed in Cairo. The next day, we went to the Egyptian Museum, and we saw the King Tutankhamun treasures. They were incredible. Then we visited the Pyramids and the Sphinx. We were tired, but the day wasn't over! After that, we flew to Luxor. The next morning, we went to the temple of Karnak. It's huge. Then we took a boat across the river. We visited the Valley of the Kings. The tomb of King Tutankhamun is there. It wasn't very interesting though. All of the treasures are in the museum in Cairo! It was also very hot in the desert, and it was crowded with tourists. Next, we returned to Cairo. The fourth day, we went to the Khan El Khalili market and bought a lot of souvenirs. It was hot and crowded, too, but finally, we relaxed. We went out on a sailboat. It's very quiet out on the Nile. It was a great trip! BTW, do you like the photos? I took them with my new digital camera. I hope you go to Egypt someday.

See you soon!
James

B ▶ Write it. Write about a trip that you took in the past.

1. Complete these sentences about a past trip. Then add time words to show the sequence.

| after that | finally | first | next | then |

TIME WORD	ACTION
	I went to
	I saw
	I bought
	I returned home
	I ate
	I visited

2. Rewrite the sentences from Activity 1 in the correct order.

3. Edit your story and discuss it with a classmate.
- Circle the words in your sentences that show the order of events.
- Share your story with your classmates. Ask your classmates for more details about their trips.

PUTTING IT TOGETHER Behind the Doors

A ► Read.

1. Look at the photo. What is the reading about? Discuss it with your classmates.

The Great Pyramid of Cheops is very large and of course, ancient. The first tourists visited it over two thousand years ago, and it is still the number one tourist site in Egypt today. Archeologists also still
5 study Cheops, but they don't find new things there very often.

In 1992, however, something amazing happened. German archeologists uncovered two tunnels deep inside the pyramid. The tunnels were not on their
10 maps. They were new discoveries! There were two small doors at the end of the tunnels. Scientists built robots and put them into the tunnels. Then, in 2001, a robot made a small hole in one of the doors and

put the camera through the hole. Were there treasures?
15 Was there only dust? No, there was another door!

Archeologists do not agree about what is behind the door. Some think that there is a library of ancient history. Others think there is a treasure, like the treasures found in the tomb of Tutankhamun. Some
20 think there is nothing behind the door. No one knows for sure. For many years, archeologists searched the pyramids, but they didn't find anything.
25 Until 1992, that is.

2. Checkpoint. Write answers to these questions.

1. Where is the Great Pyramid of Cheops? _____

2. What happened there in 1992? _____

3. Where are the doors? _____

4. What do archeologists think is behind the doors? _____

B ► Listen.

1. Listen to the conversation and check (✓) the things that Tina and Mike think are behind the door.

	Tina	Mike
1. nothing		
2. gold		
3. another door		

	Tina	Mike
4. a tomb		
5. a mummy		
6. bones		

2. Checkpoint. Who do you agree with, Tina or Mike? Why? Discuss this with the class.

C ► Wrap it up.

1. TOEFL® iBT Tina and Mike's discussion about the Pyramid of Cheops _____.

    a. describes things in the pyramid

    b. predicts what is in the pyramid

    c. describes how thieves took the treasures from the pyramid

    d. proves that archeologists know everything about Cheops

2. Write three things that you think are behind the doors. Combine your ideas with a partner's. Then rank your six ideas from the least likely (1) to most likely (6).

5 These Are a Few of My Favorite Things!

READING AND SPEAKING

A ▶ Warm up. Discuss these questions in pairs.

1. What are five things that some children collect?
2. What are five things that some adults collect?
3. Do you collect anything? If so, what's in your collection?

B ▶ Read. Look at the title and the photos in the article. Predict what it is about. Circle a, b, c, or d.

a. a new and expensive shampoo
b. an expensive haircut
c. an odd and expensive collection
d. odd hairstyles

> **TIP**
> **Possessive Adjectives:**
> *my, your, his, her, its, their, our*
> Possessive adjectives show possession or ownership. They also can show a relationship with another person. For example, *He showed **his** collection to **my** father.*

Collecting the Most Valuable Hair in the World

Connecticut businessman John Reznikoff **is crazy about** hair. In fact, he collects it. Reznikoff has a collection of hair from over 120 famous dead people. He has hair from politicians, musicians, and even
5 the actress Marilyn Monroe. Reznikoff got her hair from a doctor. This doctor cared for Monroe's body after she died. Collectible hair can be expensive. Reznikoff paid a lot of money for some of Abraham Lincoln's hair. Lincoln was president of the United States from 1861 to 1865. The hair **cost an**
10 **arm and a leg**, but Reznikoff said it was **worth every penny**. "That hair is my favorite item," he explained. So when some collectors offered him $50,000 for it, he **turned down** their offer.

Eric Gaines and his brother Mike collect hair from famous writers like Ernest Hemingway. "When we started," Eric said, "nobody else collected
15 hair. Our friends said, 'Your collection **gives us the creeps**.' But now those same people think it's cool."

Hair collecting began to **take off** in the early 1990s. It grows in popularity every day. There are more than 400 hair collectors in the United States today. There are at least 100 hair collectors in other countries.
20 This strange new hobby **is here to stay**.

⋂ A ▶ Listen.

1. Who does each item belong to? Check (✓) the items that belong to Nina or Jennifer.

Item	Nina	Jennifer
1. red pillows	☐	✓
2. lunchboxes	☐	☐
3. mugs	☐	☐
4. autographs	☐	☐
5. T-shirt	☐	☐

2. Pair Work. Look at the picture of Nina and Jennifer's room. With a partner, pretend you are Sara or Nina. Point to the items and talk about them. Use *this*, *that*, *these*, *those*, *this one* and *that one*.

Example: Sara: Are those red pillows yours?
Nina: No, those are Jennifer's.

B ▶ Interview. Write three interview questions about any topic. Use *this*, *that*, and *those*. Then interview three classmates. Complete the chart.

Example: When did you come to this school?
How much did that book cost?
Where did you buy those shoes?

Questions	Student 1	Student 2	Student 3
1. (this)			
2. (that)			
3. (those)			
4. What do you think about these questions?			

A ▶ Discuss. What do you think the man in the picture collects? Where does he buy them?

B ▶ Listen. How often does Bill look for lamps? Circle a, b, or c.

1. looks on the Internet
   a. every day   b. once a month   c. twice a week
2. goes to flea markets
   a. hardly ever   b. once a week   c. every Sunday
3. goes to thrift stores
   a. about once a week b. once a month   c. about twice a month
4. looks at catalogs
   a. every month   b. twice a year   c. hardly ever

C ▶ Listen again. Where did Bill buy his lamps? Write them in the correct category.

bicycle seat lamp	palm tree lamp	rock lamp
elephant lamp	pineapple lamp	UFO lamps

Internet	Flea Market	Mall
pineapple lamp		

Skill Focus Categorizing
We categorize things by putting them in groups. These groups share one or more common features. For example, *English*, *science*, and *history* can all be categorized as *school subjects*.

D ▶ Group work. Discuss these questions with your classmates.

1. Where do you like to shop? What do you like to buy there?
2. Complete the chart to show how often and where you shop for personal things, such as clothes, music, and books. Then share your answers with your group.

Time Expression	Item	Name or Type of Store
every day		
once a week		
once a month		
hardly ever		

∩ **A ▸ Listen and practice.** Then practice again using the other expressions.

A: I like to shop on this street.

A: Really? **Not me**. But I like to look at everything. I just don't like the prices.
* **I don't.**

B: **Me too**. I always buy something interesting.
* **So do I.**
* **I do, too.**

B: **I don't, either**. But I like the art!
* **Neither do I.**
* **Me neither.**

B ▸ Pair work. Continue these conversations with a partner. Use the expressions from Activity A to express similar and different opinions.

Example: **A:** I like shopping at thrift stores.
  B: I do, too. I always find a bargain.

1. **A:** I think laptop computers are worth every penny.
   B: . . .
2. **A:** I don't like shopping on the Internet.
   B: . . .
3. **A:** I love watching TV.
   B: . . .

C ▸ Group work. Think about things that people collect. Write five opinions about them.

Example: I don't think collecting mugs is very interesting.

1. _____
2. _____
3. _____
4. _____
5. _____

Now share your opinions with your classmates. Do they agree or disagree?

Example: **A:** I don't think collecting mugs is very interesting.
  B: Neither do I.

A ▸ Study it. Read the paragraph. Answer these questions. Circle a, b, c, or d.

1. What is the main idea?
   a. how to start a car collection
   b. Wyclef Jean's most famous motorcycle
   c. how to customize a car or motorcycle
   d. Wyclef Jean's unique car and motorcycle collection

2. Choose the best concluding sentence to put at the end of the article.
   a. Wyclef Jean loves his cars and motorcycles.
   b. There is no other collection like it in the world.
   c. His collection also includes a Ferrari 360 Spider F1.
   d. People with car collections usually collect other things as well, such as paintings or rare books.

> **Skill Focus** **The Concluding Sentence**
> A concluding sentence is usually the last sentence in a paragraph. A good concluding sentence often repeats the paragraph's main idea in different words. Look for the main idea in the topic sentence.

WYCLEF JEAN'S WHEELS

Wyclef Jean has one of the most interesting car and motorcycle collections in the world. This hip-hop singer and record producer owns 37 rare and exotic cars and motorcycles. He gives
5   each one special colors, carpeting, and extra features. His 1957 Cadillac Eldorado is painted bright pink. That is his favorite color. He also owns a $150,000 motorcycle inspired by Spider-Man, his favorite superhero. But the most
10 famous car in his collection is his 2003 Hummer H2, which has a fish tank filled with sharks.

B ▸ Write it. Write a concluding sentence.

1. Read the paragraph below. Underline the main idea.

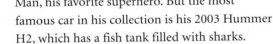

> Janet Francis wants to teach about local history. She has a collection of 50 old maps of her Boston neighborhood. She also has a collection of old photos from the neighborhood. Every month, Janet invites neighbors to her apartment to look at her maps and photos. "People like to see how this neighborhood changed," Janet says.

2. Write a concluding sentence for the paragraph. Make sure to repeat the paragraph's main idea using different words.

_____

_____

3. Read the concluding sentences of two other students. Now read your concluding sentence again. Do you want to revise it?

A ▸ Read.

1. Underline the main idea.

Lakshmi Sampath needed about $500 for a new digital camera, so she decided to sell her stamp collection. First she went to a famous stamp dealer in downtown Chicago, but she didn't trust him. "Those stamp dealers charge an
5 arm and a leg to sell your stamps," Lakshmi explained.

Lakshmi tried to sell her collection at a flea market, but nobody bought it. So she put an ad on the Internet.

After an hour, Lakshmi got an email from Daniel Hart in Anchorage, Alaska. Daniel said he wanted to buy her
10 collection. He offered her $700.

Lakshmi thought about selling her stamps. It made her sad. Some of the stamps were very important to her because they were from her father. That night, she emailed Daniel and turned down his offer.

2. Checkpoint. Write answers to these questions.

1. Why did Lakshmi want to sell her stamp collection? _____

2. Who offered to buy the collection? _____

3. Why did Lakshmi turn down his offer? _____

B ▸ Listen.

1. Read the questions about the conversation. Answer *yes* or *no*.

1. Did Daniel get any stamps from Lakshmi? _____

2. Is Daniel happy about what happened with Lakshmi? _____

2. Checkpoint. Answer the questions.

1. Why did Lakshmi turn down Daniel's first offer?
2. What was Daniel's second offer?
3. After Daniel sent Lakshmi a check, what did Lakshmi send Daniel?

C ▸ Wrap it up.

1. (TOEFL® iBT) Compare Daniel's first offer to his second offer. What was different about the second one? Why did Lakshmi accept it?

2. With a partner, look at these events from parts A and B. Put them in the correct sequence.

_____ Daniel offered to buy Lakshmi's whole collection.   _____ Lakshmi turned down Daniel's offer.

_____ Lakshmi went to a stamp dealer in Chicago.   _____ Daniel sent her a check for $500.

_____ Daniel offered to buy some of Lakshmi's stamps.   _____ Lakshmi put an ad on the Internet.

3. With your partner, read Activity A again. Then talk about what Daniel said in Activity B. Add at least three more events to the sequence above.

READING AND SPEAKING

A ▶ Warm up. With a partner, list ten technological products, or gadgets. Which ones do you use?

∩ B ▶ Read. Scan the blog, or personal Internet article, and underline the three inventions. Then circle the name of the person who wrote the blog.

Jason's Daily Blog, April 15 　　　　　　　　　　　　　　　 ⬚ ⬚ ✕

Why Didn't I Think of These?

I think these three inventions are here to stay.

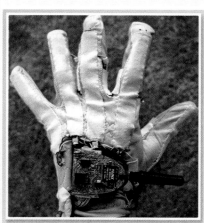

The sign language glove is a great invention for deaf people, or people who can't hear. Many deaf people can't speak clearly, so they communicate using sign language. They make words and communicate with their hands. Many people can't understand sign language, but this glove translates the sign language and **displays** the words on a small **screen**. People can carry this screen in their pocket.

The second cool invention is the laser **keyboard**. With this invention, your **cell phone** can turn into a full-size keyboard. A laser in your cell phone can display a keyboard on any table. You can type anywhere! It's easy to type **text messages** and long emails into your cell phone. It's even easy to **surf** the web and look at any **website** you want.

The third invention is the disposable cell phone, and it's my favorite. The disposable cell phone is very convenient. It is the size of a credit card, so it's easy to carry. When the battery dies, you just throw the phone away. But you can only talk on the phone for 60 minutes and you can't **recharge** the battery. A new phone costs about $20.

You can **go online** to find out more about these cool gadgets.

C ▶ Read again. Read the paragraph about the laser keyboard. Check (✓) the best summary.

    a. ____ Now you can use your cell phone like a computer. It's easy to type long emails into your cell phone.

    b. ____ The laser keyboard is a full-size keyboard for cell phones. The cell phone displays a keyboard onto any table, so you can type anywhere.

> **Skill Focus** **Summarizing**
> A summary tells the main idea. It also gives one or two important details that support the main idea.

D ▶ Group work. Take a poll.

1. What do your group members think about the inventions below? Write the total number of votes in each column.

Would you buy a _____?	Yes	No
1. sign language glove	☐	☐
2. laser keyboard	☐	☐
3. disposable cell phone	☐	☐

2. In your group, explain your answers.

▼ VOCABULARY Technology

A ▶ Identify. Circle a, b, or c to complete each sentence.

1. Sam has to _____ his cell phone because the battery is dead.
    a. recharge   b. display   c. renew

2. Anna thought the movie was boring, so she _____ the Internet instead.
    a. went online   b. surfed   c. text messaged

3. My cell phone _____ is really small, so I don't like to surf with it.
    a. screen   b. website   c. technology

4. I can't see the photos because the website doesn't _____ any of them.
    a. display   b. go online with   c. translate

B ▶ Pair work. Discuss these questions with a partner. Use the words from the box.

Nouns:	cell phone	keyboard	screen	text message	website
Verbs:	display	go online	recharge	surf	

1. Describe what each person in the picture is doing.
2. List five things people do online.

_____

_____

_____

3. What are your favorite websites? Tell why.

Modals: *Can* and *Could* for Ability

We use *can* to talk about things we know how to do or things that are possible for us to do. *Cannot* or *can't* is the negative of *can*.

Can they type on that keyboard? → Yes, they **can.** / No, they **can't.**
I **can** surf the web on my cell phone.
You **can't** download the document from the website, but I **can** email it to you.
She **can** speak Chinese, but she **can't** read it.

We use *could* to talk about things we knew how to do or things that were possible for us to do in the past. *Could not* or *couldn't* is the negative of *could*.

I **could** type on a keyboard when I was five years old.
He **couldn't** download the file two weeks ago because his computer was broken. But now his computer is fixed, so he can do it.
Nancy **could** understand Spanish two years ago, but she **couldn't** speak it very well.
I **couldn't** call because I **couldn't** recharge my cell phone.

TIP ▶ **Using *ago***
We use *ago* to talk about when things happened in the past.

I bought my laser keyboard three months **ago**.
She went online an hour **ago**.
People didn't have cell phones thirty years **ago**.
I couldn't drive a car five years **ago**.

A ▶ **Practice.** Circle the correct word.

1. I (can / can't) use this keyboard because it's too small for me.

2. My father (could / couldn't) send text messages two years ago. He didn't know how.

3. Jeong-mi is from Korea. She (can / can't) speak Korean.

4. Cell phones (can't / couldn't) display color graphics ten years ago.

5. We (can / can't) find that website. Can you help us?

B ▶ **Listen.** Circle the word that you hear.

1. can   can't

2. could   couldn't

3. can   can't

4. can't   couldn't

5. can   can't

How old is this cell phone?

A ▶ Read.

1. Read the article and complete the chart. What could the artist do in his apartment a year ago? What couldn't he do a year ago? Check (✓) each correct item.

Could Do	Couldn't Do
---------- have one person over	---------- have many of his friends over
---------- exercise	---------- exercise
---------- hang his small paintings	---------- hang his small paintings
---------- hang his big paintings	---------- hang his big paintings

He Can Put His Sofa on the Ceiling

Brian James is a painter. But now he is also an inventor. Brian makes balloon furniture. It floats on the ceiling!

5 Brian made his first balloon furniture a year ago. "I was really uncomfortable in my apartment because it was so small," Brian
10 said. "It's only one room! I could hang my small paintings, but I couldn't hang my big ones. I didn't have any room! I couldn't exercise or have a lot of friends
15 over for dinner. There was nowhere to sit! I could only have one person over at a time."

So Brian made his own furniture that could float to the
20 ceiling. "When I need to go to sleep, I pull down my bed from the ceiling. Now I can exercise in my apartment, and I can have all my friends for dinner. And I can
25 hang all my big paintings, too."

What's Brian's newest creation? A website. "Please go to my website!" Brian said. "Buy my stuff so I can move to a new
30 apartment!"

2. Pair work. Discuss your answers from number 1. Make a list of three things he can do now.

1. _____

2. _____

3. _____

B ▶ Group work. Discuss things you could and couldn't do in the past.

1. Write what you could and couldn't do in the past.

Examples: I *could stay up until 2:00* A.M. five years ago.

I *couldn't speak English* ten years ago.

What you could do:

1. I _____ five years ago.

2. I _____ ten years ago.

What you couldn't do:

3. I _____ five years ago.

4. I _____ ten years ago.

2. Tell your classmates what you could and couldn't do. Can you do it now? Use *and, so,* and *but.*

Example: I couldn't speak English ten years ago, but I can speak it fluently now.

A ▶ Discuss. Look at the photo of inventor Ryan Patterson. What is he wearing?

Name three things you already know about this invention.

1. _____

2. _____

3. _____

🎧 **B ▶ Listen.** Listen for specific information. Match the sentence beginnings and endings.

1. Cathy can only _____.

2. The workers at local restaurants _____.

3. Cathy couldn't _____.

4. The glove can _____.

a. put the words onto a screen

b. order food

c. can't understand sign language

d. communicate with sign language

🎧 **C ▶ Listen again.** Check (✓) the best summary of the listening.

a. _____ Now Cathy Parks can order food at local restaurants. Her glove helps her.

b. _____ Cathy Parks is deaf and can't speak clearly, but the sign language glove helps her communicate. Now she can communicate with anyone.

c. _____ The workers at local restaurants can't understand sign language. Now they can understand Cathy Parks.

d. _____ Cathy Parks is deaf and can't speak clearly. She can order food at local restaurants.

D ▶ Group work. Plan a talent show with your group.

1. First, discuss what each member can and can't do. Then write what they *can* do in the box. Some examples: *speak Farsi, garden, sing, teach how to make dessert.*

2. Decide what each member will do. Next decide who will present their talents first, second, third, and so on. Then practice teaching or showing the rest of the group your talent or skill.

Member's Name	What the Members Can Do

CONVERSATION STRATEGY Offering, Accepting, and Declining Invitations

🎧 **A ▶ Listen and practice.** Then practice again using the other phrases and expressions.

A: Would you like to go to Laura's party tonight?

* **Do you want to** . . .
* **Can you** . . .

A: Oh, right. Well, there's another party next week. **Would you like to** go to that one?

* **Do you want to** . . .
* **Can you** . . .

B: Sorry, I can't. I have to work on that website project for class.

* **Thanks, but I'm busy.**
* **Thanks, but I don't have time.**

B: That sounds good. Thanks!

* **That sounds great.**
* **Sure, I'd like that.**
* **Definitely.**
* **I'd love to.**

B ▶ Pair work. Continue these conversations with a partner. Use the phrases and expressions from Activity A to offer, accept, or decline invitations.

1. **A:** Do you want to come to my birthday party?
   B: Sure, . . .
2. **A:** Would you like to have dinner with us?
   B: Thanks, but . . .
3. **A:** Do you want to go to the concert with us?
   B: Sorry, . . .

C ▶ Role-play. List four things that you want to invite a partner to do. Then invite your partner. Be sure to use phrases to offer, accept, or decline invitations.

Example: concert at the student union tomorrow

_____   _____

_____   _____

A: Would you like to go to a concert at the student union tomorrow?
B: Sorry, but I can't. I need to help my brother set up his computer.
A: Okay. There's a basketball game on Friday. Do you want to go to that?
B: I'd love to.

A ▶ Study it. Read the newspaper article.

1. Circle the main idea and underline the details.

Make **Makes it Easy**

Five years ago, people couldn't find out about inventions very easily. But *Make* changed that. The *Make* magazine and website are for people who make things out of everyday items. One
5 article is about a robot made from an old cell phone. Another article tells how to make your computer screen into a TV. Inventors love *Make* because they can learn about these new
10 inventions. They can share ideas online and they can download the instructions from the *Make* website. *Make*
15 makes it easy to invent!

2. Check (✓) the best summary.

a. __ **Summary 1**

Make is a magazine and website for people who make things out of everyday items. Inventors can share ideas online and download instructions for inventions.

b. __ **Summary 2**

Make is a magazine and website that shows people how to make a robot from an old cell phone. You can download instructions from the *Make* website.

B ▶ Write it. Write a summary of the paragraph about disposable cell phones on page 46.

1. Read the paragraph about disposable cell phones.

    1. What is the main idea? _____

    2. What are two supporting details? _____

    _____

    _____

2. Write a summary of the paragraph. Use two or three sentences.

_____

_____

_____

_____

3. Edit your summary.

    • Circle the main idea.

    • Underline the other important information.

A ▸ Read.

1. Read the first paragraph and underline the main idea.

A Young Man with a Big Idea

The Million Dollar Homepage

Alex Tew was 21 and didn't have any money. He lived in England with his parents because he couldn't pay for his own apartment. He wanted to go to college, but he couldn't pay 5 for it. His mother said, "Get a job." But he needed a car to get to work, and cars are expensive. His father said, "Start your own business." But Alex didn't have money to start a business. He didn't know what to do. 10 Then Alex saw the pop-up ads on the computer. He had an idea.

2. Checkpoint. Write answers to these questions.

1. Why couldn't Alex go to college or start his own business? _____

2. Where did Alex live? _____ Who did he live with? _____

B ▸ Listen.

1. Listen and answer these questions.

1. Who is speaking? _____.

2. Where is the speaker located? _____.

2. Checkpoint. Answer these questions with a partner.

1. How did Alex make a million dollars? Describe what he did.
2. What can Alex do now that he couldn't do before?

C ▸ Wrap it up.

1. TOEFL® iBT The reading describes Alex's problem. What information does the listening tell us?

   a. more details
   b. an example of the problem
   c. a solution to the problem
   d. another problem

2. How do you think Alex's parents feel about his website? How do you think their lives are different now?

3. Imagine that you have a million dollars. What can you do with it? Can it solve your problems? Explain.

Expansion Units 4–6

A ▶ Warm up. Write a caption from the box for each photo. Then compare your captions with a partner. Which captions are the same? Which captions are different?

> Aliens from outer space? You've got to be kidding!
> I love this kind of movie.
> I never turn down a roller coaster ride!
> I think aliens are real.
>
> I think scary places are cool.
> I'm afraid of roller coasters.
> I'm not crazy about this kind of movie.
> This place gives me the creeps.

1. _____

2. _____

3. _____

4. _____

🎧 **B ▶ Listen.** Check (✓) the correct boxes for each person.

	Clara	Kim
1. stayed at grandparents' house	☐	☐
2. saw a ghost	☐	☐
3. doesn't believe in ghosts	☐	☐
4. believes in ghosts	☐	☐

> **TIP ▶** A *ghost* is the spirit of a dead person. Some people believe in ghosts, and some people don't.

C ▶ Discuss. Answer these questions with a partner.

1. With a partner, check your answers in Activity B. Ask questions about the chart using *who*.
   Example: Who stayed at her grandparents' house?
2. Why did Clara go to the kitchen?
3. Did Clara see a ghost? What do you think? Explain your answer.

D ▶ Listen again. Put these events in the order that they happened. Number them from 1 to 6.

a. ____ It was dark in the kitchen, and Clara felt very cold.

b. ____ Then Clara saw a woman in a long white gown.

c. ____ Clara decided to go to the kitchen for something to eat.

d. ____ Clara couldn't sleep.

e. ____ Clara opened the door to the kitchen.

f. ____ The woman suddenly turned around and flew out the window.

E ▶ Group work. What happened to you?

1. Think about something unusual, scary, or exciting that happened to you. Write notes in the chart.

What happened to you?	
Where?	
When?	

2. Talk about your experience in a small group. Then listen to your classmates. Fill in the chart with names.

Example: A: What happened to you?
   B: Two weeks ago, I found a wallet on the sidewalk. Inside the wallet, there was $500!
   A: You're kidding!
   B: No, it's true. And that's not all! There was a name in the wallet, and it was the name of a famous criminal.
   C: That's unbelievable. What did you do?
   B: I took the wallet to the police station.

	Classmates' names
Something unusual happened.	
Something scary happened.	
Something exciting happened.	

A ▶ Vocabulary boost! Read each sentence. Then choose the best definition for the word or expression in bold. Circle a or b.

1. These sunglasses are **all the rage** this spring.
   a. making people angry
   b. very popular

2. Frank started a very successful computer software company and **made a fortune**.
   a. was very lucky
   b. made a lot of money

3. Clothes can be of many different **materials**—cotton, wool, or other fabrics.
   a. cloth
   b. styles

4. When we go camping in the mountains, we sleep in a **tent**.
   a. a temporary fabric shelter
   b. a small cabin made of wood

5. These inexpensive shoes will **wear out** quickly. After a few weeks, they will have holes and fall apart.
   a. become useless from being used
   b. be useful outside

B ▶ Read. Look at the photos. Predict what the article is about. Circle a, b, or c.
   a. shopping for jeans
   b. the history of blue jeans
   c. jeans made in San Francisco

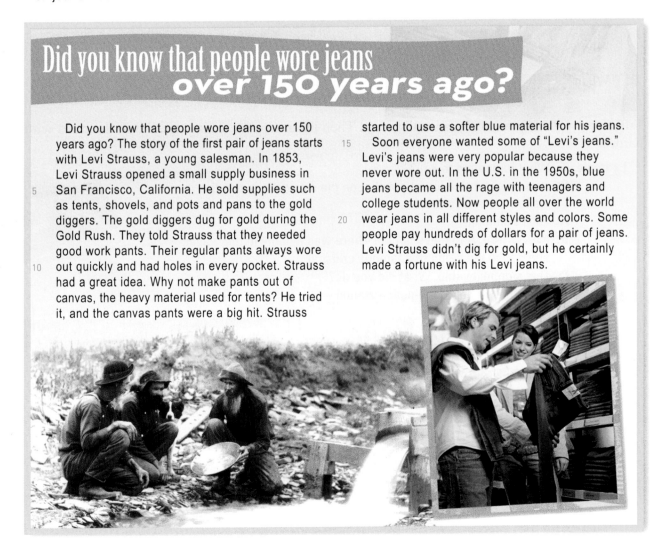

Did you know that people wore jeans *over 150 years ago?*

Did you know that people wore jeans over 150 years ago? The story of the first pair of jeans starts with Levi Strauss, a young salesman. In 1853, Levi Strauss opened a small supply business in
5 San Francisco, California. He sold supplies such as tents, shovels, and pots and pans to the gold diggers. The gold diggers dug for gold during the Gold Rush. They told Strauss that they needed good work pants. Their regular pants always wore
10 out quickly and had holes in every pocket. Strauss had a great idea. Why not make pants out of canvas, the heavy material used for tents? He tried it, and the canvas pants were a big hit. Strauss

started to use a softer blue material for his jeans.
15 Soon everyone wanted some of "Levi's jeans." Levi's jeans were very popular because they never wore out. In the U.S. in the 1950s, blue jeans became all the rage with teenagers and college students. Now people all over the world
20 wear jeans in all different styles and colors. Some people pay hundreds of dollars for a pair of jeans. Levi Strauss didn't dig for gold, but he certainly made a fortune with his Levi jeans.

C ▸ Pair work.

1. Answer these questions with a partner.

    1. Who invented jeans? _____

    2. Why did his customers like Levi's jeans? _____

    3. When did jeans become popular with teenagers? _____

2. Interview your partner and complete the chart.

Question	Answer
1. How often do you wear jeans?	
2. Why do you think jeans are popular?	
3. List five words to describe jeans.	

D ▸ Read again.
Circle the main idea and underline the important details in the article. Then check (✓) the best summary below.

    a. ____ Levi Strauss made the first jeans for gold diggers in California. Now jeans are popular all over the world.

    b. ____ Levi Strauss made the first jeans from canvas. Now some people pay hundreds of dollars for a pair of jeans.

E ▸ Write about it.

1. Read the paragraph below and underline the main idea. Then write a concluding sentence. Repeat the main idea using different words.

> Most young people enjoy wearing jeans. There are several reasons for the popularity of jeans. First, they are usually inexpensive. The low cost is important for students and young people. Second, jeans come in a variety of styles and colors. Last, jeans are very comfortable to wear. _____
>
> _____
>
> _____

2. Compare your concluding sentence with a partner's sentence. Do you want to revise your sentence?

7 Good, Better, Best

READING AND SPEAKING

A ▶ Warm up. Discuss in pairs.

1. Name three difficult sports. Why are they difficult?

2. How much strength do you think basketball requires? Circle a number from 1 to 10.

1	2	3	4	5	6	7	8	9	10
no strength				**medium strength**				**a lot of strength**	

3. Now think about the three sports you named in question 1. Rate them with a partner.

B ▶ Read. Skim the article and the graph. Underline the names of sports. Then answer these questions.

1. Which sport got an intelligence score over 7?
   a. boxing   b. soccer   c. tennis

2. Which sport got a strength score over 8?
   a. gymnastics   b. surfing   c. boxing

> **Skill Focus** **Using a Graph to Aid Comprehension**
> Graphs contain additional information that supports ideas in a reading. They are usually more specific than the reading.

The Most Difficult Sport in the World

What is the hardest sport in the world?

A group of sports experts rated the difficulty of six different sports. The experts looked at a combination of intelligence and strength. They
5   gave each category a rating of 1 to 10.

Based on their study, the experts decided that soccer players have to be smarter than other athletes. Soccer got an intelligence score of 7.5 but a strength score of only 4.1. **Boxing** got a
10 strength score of 8.1, but a much lower intelligence score.

Not everyone thinks the list is helpful. College student Lisa Hamlin plays **basketball** and **surfs**, and she thinks the list is too short.
15 "There aren't enough sports on the list," said Lisa. "My friends **play baseball** and **go horseback riding** and play **golf**. Why aren't those sports on the list?"

20 But Jake Madding, a 23-year-old college student, agrees with the list. "I don't box, so I don't know how much strength it takes. But I play soccer and I also **do gymnastics**, and I think gymnasts have to be stronger than soccer players. Gymnastics is a hard sport."

25 But is it the hardest? The experts added their scores for strength and intelligence. Surfing had the lowest score, and boxing had the highest. Boxing is the hardest sport in the world.

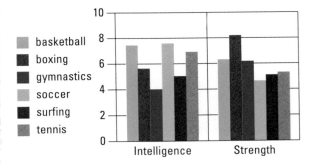

C ▶ Read again. Check (✓) True or False.

		True	False
1.	The experts said surfing is the hardest sport.	☐	☐
2.	Tennis got a strength score of 6.2.	☐	☐
3.	Basketball got a high intelligence score.	☐	☐
4.	Soccer got a low strength score.	☐	☐
5.	Jake Madding doesn't box, but he plays soccer.	☐	☐

D ▶ Pair work. Discuss these questions with your partner.

1. According to the article, what is the most difficult sport? What is difficult about it?
2. Make a bar graph comparing swimming, volleyball, and baseball. Give each a score for intelligence and strength.

VOCABULARY Verbs with Sports and Activities

do	gymnastics, homework
go	golfing, horseback riding, jogging, running, skiing, surfing, swimming
play	baseball, basketball, golf, soccer, tennis, volleyball, the piano, the drums, the guitar
(X)	box, golf, jog, run, ski, surf, swim (These words **are** the verbs.)

A ▶ Identify. Complete the sentences with the correct form of the verb *go, play,* or *do*. Write an *X* in the blank if no verb is needed.

1. Do you _____ horseback riding in the morning?

2. She wants to learn how to _____ box.

3. Can you _____ the piano? I _____ the drums.

4. Before Francisco _____ basketball, he _____ his homework.

5. Jason likes to _____ tennis, but Jenn likes to _____ ski.

B ▶ Pair work. Discuss these questions with a partner.

1. Name four sports and activities that you like. Why do you like them? Then name four different sports and activities that you don't like. Tell why.
2. Rate the strength and intelligence required for each sport and activity you named above. Use numbers 1–10. Explain your ratings to your partner.

GETTING INTO GRAMMAR

Comparative and Superlative Forms of Adjectives

The **comparative form** of an adjective is used to compare two things. We use *than* between the adjective and the noun.

We use *–er* for adjectives with one syllable. When an adjective ends in a vowel + a consonant, we add another consonant before the *–er:* big / big**ger**; hot / hot**ter**; sad / sad**der**.

> Gymnasts have to be strong**er than** soccer players. Miami is hot**ter than** Seattle.
> Lenny is tall, but Michael is tall**er than** Lenny.

We use *–ier* for adjectives that end in *y*.

> Golf and baseball are eas**ier than** soccer. Boxers are usually heav**ier than** gymnasts.

We use *more* + **adjective** for longer adjectives.

> They said that soccer players have to be **more intelligent than** other athletes.

The **superlative form** of an adjective is used to compare more than two things. We use *the* before the adjective.

We use *–est* for adjectives with one syllable.

> Boxing is **the** hard**est** sport in the world.

We use *–iest* for adjectives that end in *y*.

> I think the drums are **the** eas**iest** instrument to play. I think anyone can play them.

We use *the most* + **adjective** for adjectives with more than one syllable.

> What is **the most difficult** sport in the world?

Irregular Forms

Good and *bad* have irregular forms: *good, better, best / bad, worse, worst*

> She is a **good** coach, but Coach Chase is **better**. And Coach Foster is the **best**.
> I'm a **bad** skier, but my mom is **worse**. And my dad is the **worst!** He always falls!

A ▶ Practice. Find and correct the errors. One sentence is correct.

1. That building is the prettier in the city. _____

2. Reese Witherspoon is a good actor, but I think Scarlett Johansson is better. _____

3. This room is hot, but that one is hoter and more small. _____

4. It's the worstest restaurant in the city! _____

5. This is the most comfortable and expensivest sofa in the whole store. _____

B ▶ Pair work. Complete the sentences with your own ideas. Read them to a partner.

1. My father is _____shorter_____ than my mother.

2. My best friend is _____ than I am.

3. I think _____ is the most _____ country in the world.

4. English is _____ than _____.

5. Text messages are _____ than _____.

6. _____ is good, _____ is better, and _____ is the best.

🎧 **A ▶ Read and listen.**

1. Read and try to complete each sentence with a comparative or superlative. Then listen and check your answers.

   1. The _____ professional basketball player in U.S. history was Jermaine O'Neal. He was 18 years old when he started playing for the Portland Trail Blazers team.

   2. Many people think Babe Didrikson Zaharias was the _____ _____ female athlete in history. She played golf and many other sports.

   3. Robert Wadlow was _____ _____ man in the world. He was eight feet and eleven inches (2.7 meters) tall. Robert's mother and father were much _____ than he was.

   4. Fuatai Solo is the _____ coconut tree climber in the world. He climbed a 30-foot (9-meter) tree in 4.88 seconds.

   5. Alice Walton is the _____ woman in the world. Her father started Wal-Mart stores. She is _____ than England's Queen Elizabeth.

Jermaine O'Neal

Babe Didrikson Zaharias

Robert Wadlow

2. Pair work. Talk about the people above with your partner. Ask questions about them using comparatives and superlatives.

> **Examples:** Who do you think is the most interesting?
> Who is richer than Queen Elizabeth?

B ▶ Interview. Read the questions and write three more. Use comparatives and superlatives. Interview two classmates and compare their answers.

Questions	Student 1:_____.	Student 2:_____.
1. Are you shorter or taller than your best friend?		
2. Who is the most interesting person you know?		
3.		
4.		
5.		

A ▶ **Discuss.** Look at the photos. Which place looks the most interesting?

🎧 **B** ▶ **Listen.** Listen to the couple talk about the city and the suburbs, and then write the pros (positive things) and cons (negative things) for each place. Use the words from the box.

best	cheaper	dirtiest	lonelier	noisy
better	cleaner	harder	more interesting	quieter

	Suburbs	City
Pros	1. The suburbs are so much _____ than the city. 2. It's _____ to live in the suburbs. 3. The air is _____ .	1. The city is _____ than the suburbs. 2. Restaurants are much_____ than restaurants in the suburbs. 3. Our_____ friends live in the city.
Cons	1. It's _____ in the suburbs. 2. It's a lot _____ to find good stores in the suburbs.	1. The city is really_____ , especially at night. 2. This city is the_____ place to live in the whole world!

🎧 **C** ▶ **Listen again.** Listen for Judy and Frank's tone. Check (✓) the tone for each line.

1. Hi, Judy. I didn't think you were home.
   ✓ happy ___ angry ___ sad

2. Can you hear that, Frank?
   ___ happy ___ angry ___ sad

3. I really want to move somewhere quieter.
   ___ happy ___ angry ___ sad

4. Really? Tomorrow night?
   ___ happy ___ angry ___ sad

5. Yeah, I don't want to move far away from them.
   ___ happy ___ angry ___ sad

Skill Focus **Recognizing tone**
Tone is the feeling or attitude expressed in a person's speech.

D ▶ **Pair work.** Compare life in the city, the suburbs, and the country. Write pros and cons for each.

	City	Suburbs	Country
Pros			
Cons			

∩ **A** ▶ **Listen and practice.** Then practice again using the other words and expressions.

A: This apartment is **so cool!** It's so big, and it's in the best part of the city.

* really great.
* amazing.

B: Yeah, but it's really noisy…

A: Do you think so? I think it's quieter than the other apartment. And **I love** this view. You can see the whole city!

* I really like …
* I'm really into …

B: That is pretty cool. All right, let's take it.

A: **Really**? I can't believe you said yes!

* Seriously?
* Do you mean it?
* Great!

B ▶ **Pair work.** Continue these conversations with a partner. Use the words and expressions from Activity A to express excitement and enthusiasm.

1. **A:** This Japanese restaurant looks _____. Let's go there.
   B: . . .

2. **A:** My friend said Argentina is _____. He lived in Buenos Aires for three years.
   B: . . .

3. **A:** I got tickets to the opera!
   B: . . .

C ▶ **Group work.** Make a list of five things you think are really amazing. Then tell your classmates about them. Be sure to use phrases to express excitement and enthusiasm.

1. _____.

2. _____.

3. _____.

4. _____.

5. _____.

A ▸ Study it. Read the article.

1. Who does the writer say was the smartest person in history? _____

2. Circle the main idea. Underline the examples that support the main idea.

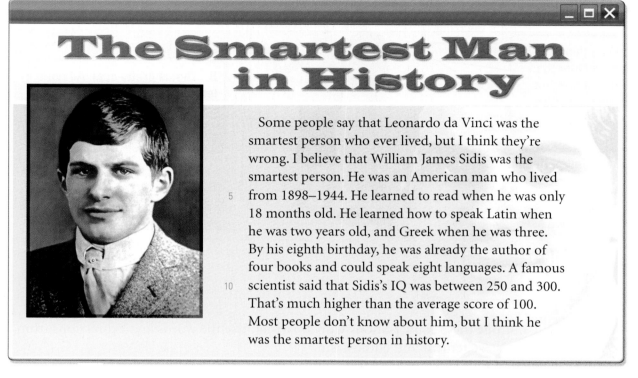

The Smartest Man in History

Some people say that Leonardo da Vinci was the smartest person who ever lived, but I think they're wrong. I believe that William James Sidis was the smartest person. He was an American man who lived
5 from 1898–1944. He learned to read when he was only 18 months old. He learned how to speak Latin when he was two years old, and Greek when he was three. By his eighth birthday, he was already the author of four books and could speak eight languages. A famous
10 scientist said that Sidis's IQ was between 250 and 300. That's much higher than the average score of 100. Most people don't know about him, but I think he was the smartest person in history.

B ▸ Write it. Write a paragraph about the smartest person that you know.

1. Complete the mind map of the smartest person that you know. Write his or her name in the middle circle. In the other circles, write at least four reasons or examples to support your opinion.

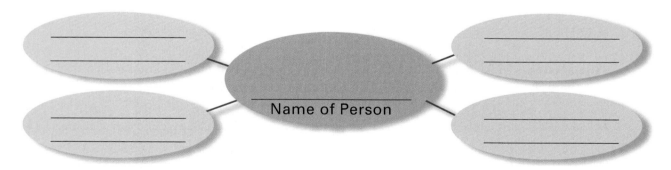

Name of Person

2. Choose three examples from your mind map. Write your paragraph.

3. Edit your paragraph.

- Circle the main idea. Underline the examples that support the main idea.
- Do your examples show how smart that person is?

A ▶ Read.

1. Which animal in the reading is the most dangerous? How many people does it kill each year?

The Most Dangerous Animals

There are some studies about the world's most dangerous animals. The results are surprising to some people. Many people think that snakes and sharks are the deadliest animals in the world, but in fact, mosquitoes kill far more people each year. Mosquitoes carry diseases that kill
5   2,000,000 people each year. When a mosquito bites a person, it can pass diseases into the person's blood. Dogs also can pass diseases through bites. Some dogs carry the disease called rabies, which kills about 40,000 people each year. Sharks, on the other hand, kill only six people each year. Which of these are you afraid of?

	dog attacks/rabies
40,000	
6	shark attacks
2,000,000	mosquito bites
125,000	snake attacks

0   500,000   1,000,000   1,500,000   2,000,000

2. Checkpoint. Write the answers to these questions.

   1. Why are the study's results surprising to some people? _____

   2. Which animals kill more people in a year, dogs or sharks? _____

   3. Which animals described in the reading can spread disease through their bite? _____

B ▶ Listen.

1. A man is giving his opinion about a dangerous animal. Who is he talking to? Circle a, b, or c.
   a. an animal expert   b. a news reporter   c. a police officer

2. Checkpoint. Write the answers to these questions.

   1. What did the man see? _____

   2. What did the man do after he saw the attack? _____

   3. According to the man, which animal is the deadliest? How many people does he say it kills each year?

   _____

C ▶ Wrap it up.

1. (TOEFL® iBT) What information from the reading and the chart contradicts the man's opinion in the listening?

2. Which other animals do you think are dangerous? What do you think can be done to make people safer from dangerous animals?

8 Trends

▼ READING AND SPEAKING

A ▶ Warm up. Discuss in pairs.

1. What clothes are very trendy, or stylish, now?
2. Name three trends from your childhood.
3. What current trends do you like? What current trends do you dislike?

🎧 **B ▶ Read.** Skim the blog and check (✓) the two trends that Amanda writes about.

___ eating out   ___ living in New York

___ really long hair   ___ really short hair

___ paper shoes   ___ cooking at home

Amanda's Blog, October 9   ⬓ ⬚ ✖

Hi Everyone!

My life is crazier than ever. I'm living in New York now, and I'm working for Coolhunter.com. I'm a trend hunter. It's really fun, but it's **wearing** me **out!** I have to work late every day. Tonight, I'm working at home because I'm doing Internet research. I'm **figuring out** what the new fashion trends are. I **found out**
5 that paper shoes are the hot new thing. Isn't that weird? The shoes are made of thick paper. They're cheap, but they only last a couple of weeks! You can't wear them when you **work out** at the gym, because they fall apart!

Last week, I had to find out what the new dining trends are. The big trend is to
10 **eat out.** Did you know that 64 percent of people between 20 and 30 go to restaurants four times a week? I can't believe how much money people spend on eating out! I'm glad I don't spend that much eating out. You all know me: I'm a homebody.
15 I don't like to **go out** that much anyway. I like to **have** people **over** and make a big dinner. When I lived in Buenos Aires, I cooked for everyone! I miss those days.
20 Actually, I'm feeling a little homesick right now. Does anyone want to come visit? **Think** it **over!**

C ▶ Read again. From the context in the reading, circle the best definition for the words.

1. homebody
   a. someone who likes to stay home
   b. someone who goes to a lot of parties
2. homesick
   a. to be very sick at home
   b. to feel sad when away from home

B ▶ Pair work. Discuss these questions with a partner.

1. What kind of person makes a good trend hunter? Name five characteristics.
2. Do you think you can be a trend hunter? Tell why.
3. Do you follow trends? Tell why.

VOCABULARY Phrasal Verbs with *out* and *over*

A ▶ Identify. Read these phrasal verbs from the blog. Circle the correct meaning.

1. wear out
   a. make tired   b. buy clothes
2. figure out
   a. understand; solve a problem   b. draw a picture
3. find out
   a. read about   b. learn; discover
4. work out
   a. go to work   b. exercise
5. eat out
   a. eat in a restaurant   b. eat food at home
6. go out
   a. leave one's house to do something   b. stay home
7. have over
   a. invite someone to one's home   b. have coffee in a restaurant
8. think over
   a. forget   b. think about

Is she worn out?

Are they eating out?

B ▶ Pair work. Discuss these questions.

1. Do you prefer to eat out or eat at home? Discuss the pros and cons of each.
2. How do people your age work out? What is the most popular form of exercise?
3. What things wear you out? What do you do when you feel worn out?

TIP Some phrasal verbs can be separated. *Figure out, find out, have over, think over,* and *wear out* are sometimes separated. Here are some examples:
   She is **figuring out** what the new fashion trends are. / She is **figuring** it **out**.
   I **found out** that paper shoes are the hot new thing. / I **found** that **out** yesterday.
   The job **wears out** the employees. / The job **wears** them **out**.
Go out and *work out* (when *work out* means "exercise") cannot be separated.

The Present Continuous

We use the present continuous to talk about what's happening now. The present continuous form uses *be* + (verb) *-ing*.

> We**'re wearing** the same shirt!
> Can I call you back later? **I'm watching** a great fashion show.
> My parents **are using** the car now, so can you pick me up?
> **Are** you **reading** that magazine now?
> Who is she **waiting** for?

We often use these words with the present continuous: *currently, now, right now.*

Some verbs are almost never used in the present continuous tense. Here are a few: *hear, like, love, need, remember, smell, taste, understand,* and *want.*

A ▸ Practice. Complete the sentences using the present continuous of the verbs in parentheses.

1. I (study) _____ for tomorrow's exam right now.

2. He (work out) _____ at the gym a lot these days.

3. Currently, they (drive) _____ an electric car from Los Angeles to San Francisco.

4. We (write) _____ a report about technology trends for our class.

5. _____ you (get) _____ wet? Please use my umbrella.

B ▸ Read. Complete the letter. Circle the correct verb.

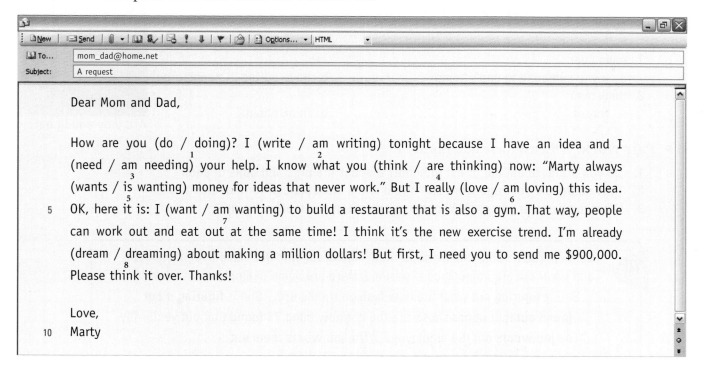

Dear Mom and Dad,

How are you (do / doing)? I (write / am writing) tonight because I have an idea and I
1
(need / am needing) your help. I know what you (think / are thinking) now: "Marty always
3   2
(wants / is wanting) money for ideas that never work." But I really (love / am loving) this idea.
                4   5
OK, here it is: I (want / am wanting) to build a restaurant that is also a gym. That way, people
                6
can work out and eat out at the same time! I think it's the new exercise trend. I'm already
              7
(dream / dreaming) about making a million dollars! But first, I need you to send me $900,000.
8
Please think it over. Thanks!

Love,
Marty

▼ ACTIVATING GRAMMAR

🎧 **A ▶ Listen and write.**

1. Check (✓) the location of each fitness trend.

Trend	Chicago	Tokyo	Bogota	Paris
1. Working out in the cold	☐	☐	☐	☐
2. Brazilian dancing	☐	☐	☐	☐
3. Indian dancing	☐	☐	☐	☐
4. Yoga in hot rooms (bikram yoga)	☐	☐	☐	☐

2. Pretend you are working out in each of the four places. For each place, write two sentences describing what you, or others, are doing. Use the present progressive.

Chicago: _I'm jogging in the snow._ _____

_____

_____

Tokyo: _____

_____

_____

Bogota: _____

_____

_____

Paris: _____

_____

_____

B ▶ Group work.

1. Look through a magazine with your group. Discuss what people are doing in the advertisements and articles. Identify four trends.

_____   _____

_____   _____

2. What do you think about these trends? Discuss your opinion with your group.

A ▶ Discuss. Look at the three photos. Describe how these people are living. What are the differences in their lifestyles?

Photo A

Photo B

Photo C

> **TIP** We also use the present continuous to talk about trends that continue over periods of time. We can use *now, these days,* and *nowadays* with this use of the present continuous.
> • People are wearing bright colors **these days.**
> • Young people are eating out three or four times a week **nowadays.**

 B ▶ Listen. Check (✓) the statements that are true about current trends in Argentina.

1. In Argentina, more young people . . .
    ____ are living at home until they get married.
    ____ are living by themselves in small apartments.
    ____ are living with older people.

2. In Argentina, many divorced people . . .
    ____ are moving to different countries.
    ____ are living with their grandparents.
    ____ are living alone.

3. In Argentina, more older people . . .
    ____ are getting divorced.
    ____ are spending many years living alone.
    ____ are buying big houses.

C ▶ Listen again. Check (✓) the sentence that gives the best gist of the news report.

    a. ____ In Argentina, many people are living alone these days.

    b. ____ In Argentina, older people are living alone.

    c. ____ More young people are living alone in Argentina.

> **Skill Focus** **Listening for Gist**
> The gist of a listening is similar to the main idea of a reading. The gist is the most important idea in a conversation or speech. To determine the gist, listen to the details and identify their common idea.

D ▶ Pair work.

1. Think of a country that you know very well. Check (✓) the statements that describe current trends there. Write two more true statements about that country.

    Country: _____

    1. ____ Most 20-year-olds are living with their parents.

    2. ____ Most 20-year-olds are living alone these days.

    3. ____ Most 70-year-olds are living in extended family homes nowadays.

    4. _____

    5. _____

2. Ask your partner about his or her answers above.

    Example: **A:** Are most 20-year-olds living alone these days?
                B: No, most are still living with their parents.

∩ **A** ▶ **Listen and practice.** Then practice again using the other phrases.

A: Hi, Do you need something?

A: Sure, go ahead.

A: Um, I don't know.

A: No, sorry. I took it off. I don't like labels!

B: Well, yes I'm a trend hunter. **May I** ask you some questions about your personal style?

* **Can I . . .**
* **Could I please . . .**
* **Is it all right if I . . .**

B: Great. I love your shirt. **Could you please** tell me the brand name?

* **Would you . . .**
* **Would you please . . .**
* **Can you . . .**

B: Oh, well, I know how to find out. May I look at the label?

B ▶ **Pair work.** Continue these conversations with a partner. Use the phrases from Activity A to ask for permission and make requests. Then switch roles.

1. **A:** Excuse me. _____ ask you some questions about this school?

   B: Sure, go ahead.

   A: . . .

2. **A:** Excuse me. _____ tell me where I could find some cool clothes?

   B: Yeah. The best place is . . .

3. **A:** _____ tell me where you like to eat?

   B: Sure. I like to go . . .

4. **A:** _____ borrow $20?

   B: Um . . .

C ▶ **Role-play.** Role-play these situations with your partner. Be sure to ask for permission and make requests using the phrases above.

1. You and your partner are trend hunters. You like each other's music and want to borrow some CDs.

2. One of you is a waiter and the other is a customer. The customer wants to ask some questions about the food before he or she orders.

3. You and your partner are roommates. One of you is hot and wants to open the window.

A ▸ Study it. Study the article excerpt.

1. What place is described in the excerpt? _____

2. Underline the sentences that give details about the place.

3. Look at the sentences you underlined. Check (✓) the different kinds of information they give.

  ___ how something looks (visual information)

  ___ how something sounds (audio information)

  ___ how something smells

  ___ how something feels when you touch it

  ___ how something tastes

  ___ information about a person (height, weight, age, hair color)

  ___ information about a place's history

> **TIP** Good descriptive writing gives a variety, or range, of details. These details can give information about how a place looks, sounds, and smells. The details might also tell about the place's history or the people you might see there.

COOL PLACES YOU SHOULD KNOW ABOUT

We are always looking for cool new travel destinations. This month, we're focusing on South America. These spots are so cool right now, they're hot!

Mancora, Peru. This small beach town in northern Peru is like a piece of paradise. Beautiful white sand beaches stretch along the bright blue Pacific Ocean. The water is cool and the sun is hot. Traditional Peruvian music plays in all the restaurants, where you can order spicy fish in lime or lemon juice (*ceviche*) and sweet fruit juices. Suntanned tourists from all over the world come here to relax in their shorts, sandals, and T-shirts. If you're looking for a cheap place to surf, eat out, and meet interesting people, this is the place for you.

B ▸ Write it. Write a descriptive paragraph about a place that is getting trendy. It can be a city, a restaurant, a store, or a country.

1. Think of the place that you're going to write about. Make notes about important details that describe the place. Circle the three most important details. Remember to include different kinds of information.

  Place: _____

  Details: _____ _____

  _____ _____

  _____ _____

  _____ _____

2. Write the paragraph. Tell the main idea in the topic sentence. Then use each detail in its own sentence.

3. Edit your paragraph.

  • Do you have at least three supporting details? Underline them. Do they give a variety of information?

A ▶ Read.

1. What type of article is this?
Circle a, b, or c.
   a.   an interview
   b.   a restaurant review
   c.   a movie review

2. Checkpoint. Answer the questions.
   1.   What kind of restaurant is Kuro?
   _____
   2.   What dishes does the reviewer like?
   _____
   3.   What dish does the reviewer dislike?
   Tell why._____
   _____

 B ▶ Listen.

1. Listen to Becky Jordan. What is her job
at Food TV? _____

2. Checkpoint. Write answers to these questions.

   1.   What food is popular with many women now? _____
   2.   What is the most popular new food category? _____
   3.   Why do some people in Japan drink black sesame water? _____

C ▶ Wrap it up.

1. [TOEFL® iBT] The trend hunter gives several examples of black foods. What dishes at the restaurant
Kuro support her idea that black foods are popular?
_____   _____

2. [TOEFL® iBT] What dish at Kuro supports the trend hunter's idea that healthy foods are popular?
_____

3. Do you want to eat at Kuro? Tell why or why not.

4. Do you eat any black foods? If so, what kinds? What kinds of healthy foods do you eat?

Kuro
Palermo SoHo, Buenos Aires

*Kuro is a new Asian restaurant with the longest menu in
Buenos Aires. I'm not kidding: this menu can wear you out.*

But it's worth it. Kuro's food is interesting, complicated, and
delicious. And it's not like anything else in this city. The chef,
5 Akira Kumagai, is using healthy ingredients that I didn't even
know about. For example, the Kuro Salad has black soybeans
in it, and has a black sesame dressing. It's surprising and very
good. In another delicious dish called Kuro Chicken, the chef
pours black vinegar over a big piece of juicy chicken and then
10 covers it with thin slices of apple. Even the dessert is healthy.
Kuro's most popular dessert is orange ice cream. It has 24
vitamins in it, but I think it's boring. It doesn't have
enough flavor!

Kuro makes eating out in Buenos Aires more fun than ever.

9

Making Connections

READING AND SPEAKING

A ▶ Warm up. Complete the chart. List three people you know outside of school. How did you meet? Are they close friends or casual acquaintances (people you don't know very well)?

Names of Three People You Know Outside of School	How You Met	Close Friend (3)	Casual Acquaintance (3)
1.			
2.			
3.			

B ▶ Read. Read the question. Then skim the article quickly and make an inference to answer the question. Circle a, b, or c.

According to the article, why is it useful to have casual acquaintances?

    a. Casual acquaintances can often become close friends.

    b. We can connect with a lot of different people through casual acquaintances.

    c. Casual acquaintances email a lot of jokes and pictures.

Are You Connected?

Email is a great way to communicate with friends and family. We can share jokes, pictures, and the latest **news** almost instantly. But it also connects us to **strangers**. Any email you send could reach someone you don't
5　know in a few minutes—on the other side of the world!

In a recent **study**, scientists asked 24,000 men and women to try to get an email to one of 18 target people in 13 countries. The **participants** did not know the email addresses of the target people, so they sent one
10　email to someone they did know. They asked that person to forward the email to someone who might know one of the targets, and so on.

Only 384 emails reached their targets. But the **research** showed some important **information**.
15　First, it didn't take much **time** for the successful emails to reach the targets. In fact, they reached their targets in about four emails. Second, most of the people between the original email **sender** and the target were not close friends of the original sender or the
20　target. They were casual **acquaintances**. This is because our close friends often know the same people that we know. But casual acquaintances know different people. This knowledge is valuable because it tells us that our casual acquaintances are important
25　to us. They can help us find **work** by telling us about jobs, and they can also introduce us to new people. They can connect us to the rest of the world.

C ▶ Read again. Sequence these events in the order that they happened. Number them from 1 (what happened first) to 5 (what happened last).

a. _____ People received emails and forwarded them to others.

b. _____ 384 emails reached their targets.

c. _____ Researchers asked 24,000 people to send emails to targets.

d. _____ Scientists learned that casual acquaintances are important.

e. _____ Participants sent emails.

Photo A

D ▶ Discuss. Ask and answer these questions with a partner.

1. Describe each photo. How are these people communicating?
2. Talk about how you communicate with close friends, casual acquaintances, and strangers.

Photo B   Photo C

VOCABULARY Count and Noncount Nouns

A ▶ Identify. Write these words from the article in the correct column in the chart.

| acquaintance | news | research | stranger | time |
| information | participant | sender | study | work |

Count Nouns	Noncount Nouns

B ▶ Pair work. Complete these questions with the correct form of the words from Activity A. Then ask and answer with a partner.

1. How much _____ do you spend reading and sending email every day?

2. Do you ever read emails from _____, or do you only read emails when you know the _____?

3. Researchers found that casual _____ can connect us to people we don't know. Why is this important?

4. Scientists have to find a lot of _____ to do a study. They have to read and do experiments. Do you have to do _____ for your classes?

5. Were you ever part of a scientific _____, or were you ever a _____ in a survey?

6. How do you find out about what's happening in the world? Do you read the newspaper, watch TV, or read the _____ online?

Expressions of Quantity to Express a Number or an Amount

We use *no, not any, any, some,* and *a lot of* with both count and noncount nouns.

> **Some** emails* reached their targets.
>
> The scientists found out **a lot of** important information from the study.
>
> I don't open **any** email messages from strangers.
>
> There are **not any** new people in this class. / There are **no** new people in this class.

We use numbers, *a few,* and *several* only with count nouns.

> I sent an email invitation to **five** good friends and **several** casual acquaintances.

We use *a little* only with noncount nouns.

> She spilled **a little** water on her computer.
>
> I get **a little** email* on the weekends and a lot on weekdays.

We use *How many* and *How much* to ask about quantity. We use *How many* with plural count nouns.

> **How many** emails did you get? → I got a lot of emails.

We use *How much* with noncount nouns.

> **How much** time do you have? → I have a little time.

*Note that *email* can be both a count and a noncount noun.

A ▶ Practice. Read the questions. Circle the correct choice in parentheses.

1. How (much / many) time do you spend sending email?

2. How (much / many) emails do you get each day?

3. How (much / many) email do you send each day?

4. How (much / many) hours do you spend online each day?

5. How (much / many) people do you communicate with each day, in person and online?

B ▶ Pair work. In the chart, write your answers to the questions from Activity A. Then ask your partner the questions and write his or her answers.

My Answers	My Partner's Answers
1.	1.
2.	2.
3.	3.
4.	4.
5.	5.

∩ A ▶ Listen and write.

1. Listen to Jack and Melissa's conversation.
Check (✓) True or False for each sentence.

	True	False
1. Jack met Melissa in high school.	☐	☐
2. Jack met Carrie in a painting class.	☐	☐
3. Jack lived in New York for a long time.	☐	☐
4. Melissa lived in New York longer than Jack did.	☐	☐
5. Jack doesn't have any paintings at the Mason Gallery.	☐	☐
6. Jack has several paintings at the Mason Gallery.	☐	☐
7. Jack has a lot of paintings at the Finch Gallery.	☐	☐
8. Jack doesn't have any paintings at the Finch gallery.	☐	☐

2. Pair work. Complete the questions and answers about Jack and Melissa. Use the nouns in parentheses in the questions and expressions of quantity in the answers. Then ask and answer the questions with a partner.

1. Question: (years) _____

Answer: Jack lived in New York for _____ years.

2. Question: (time) _____

Answer: Melissa spent _____ time in New York—about three years.

3. Question: (work) _____

Answer: Yes, Jack has _____ work at the Mason Gallery.

4. Question: (paintings) _____

Answer: No, Jack doesn't have _____ paintings in San Francisco.

B ▶ Write and talk.
On a separate piece of paper, write five questions and answers about the picture. Use *How much/How many* and expressions of quantity. Then ask and answer your questions with a partner.

How many jars of coffee are in the picture? → There are two jars of coffee in the picture.

LISTENING AND SPEAKING Believe It or Not

A ▶ Discuss. Match each topic to the correct picture. Write a, b, or c.

a. Candy + Cola = Death!   b. Gas Station Warning   c. Cell Phone Danger

1. ____   2. ____   3. ____

∩ B ▶ Listen. Check (✓) True or False for each statement about Erika and Tim.

	True	False
1. Erika gets a lot of urban legend emails.	☐	☐
2. Sometimes urban legends are true.	☐	☐
3. Tim never believes urban legends.	☐	☐
4. Erika thinks that people don't believe urban legends.	☐	☐
5. Erika thinks that people probably send urban legend emails to their friends because they want to warn them.	☐	☐

∩ C ▶ Listen again. Do Erika and Tim believe the urban legends? Complete the chart.

Urban Legends	Real or Hoax		Who said it? (Write *Tim* or *Erika*.)
	Tim	**Erika**	
1. Cell Phone Danger	Hoax		_____: You're not going to believe this one. _____: I think that might be true.
2. Gas Station Warning			_____: I hope that isn't true, but I think it is. _____: Me too.
3. Candy + Cola = Death!			_____: That's not true. That's a hoax. _____: I agree.

D ▶ Group work.

1. These words are common in urban legends in the U.S. Match each word with its definition.

1. ____ poison
2. ____ pin
3. ____ flesh
4. ____ bacteria
5. ____ razor blade
6. ____ lick

a. a thin, sharp piece of metal used for sewing
b. the soft part of your body under the skin
c. something that can make you sick or kill you if you eat it or drink it
d. a flat, sharp piece of metal used for shaving
e. to move your tongue over something to taste it or wet it
f. tiny living things that can make you sick if they get inside your body

2. Tell the class an urban legend that you know, or create a new one. Then answer these questions.

Which urban legend do you think is the scariest? _____ The funniest? _____

The most believable? _____ The least believable? _____

🎧 **A** ▶ **Listen and practice.** Then practice again using the other phrases and expressions.

A: In my opinion, the story about cell phone danger is true.

* **I think . . .**
* **I believe . . .**
* **I feel . . .**

A: What do you think about the boy who died eating fizzy candy and drinking cola?

* **How do you feel about . . .?**
* **What's your opinion on . . .?**
* **What's your feeling about . . .?**

B: Really? **I don't think** it's true. I think it's a hoax.

* **I don't believe . . .**
* **I don't feel . . .**

B: Oh, I don't think that one is true either.

B ▶ **Pair work.** Continue these conversations with a partner. Use the phrases and expressions from Activity A to ask for and give your opinion.

1. **A:** Did you hear about the danger of cell phones at gas stations?
   B: Yeah, I got that email. I . . .

2. **A:** My friend called me yesterday from Japan. She told me an amazing story!
   B: Oh really, what was it about?
   A: It was about poison in ketchup bottles.
   B: . . .

3. **A:** Did you get that email from Anna?
   B: Yeah. It said that eating shrimp and vitamin C together could make you really sick or even kill you!
   A: . . .

4. **A:** A woman died because there were spiders living in her hair.
   B: Really?
   A: . . .

C ▶ **Group work.** What do you think? Check (✓) Real or Hoax for each legend. Then discuss your answers with your classmates. Be sure to ask for and give your opinion. (See answers at the bottom of page 81.)

	Real	Hoax
1. Don't lick the deposit envelopes at your bank! They're covered in poison!	☐	☐
2. Bananas from South America have flesh-eating bacteria in them.	☐	☐
3. Pins and razor blades were found in holiday candy in the U.S.	☐	☐

A ▶ **Study it.** Read the email.

1. Circle the main idea.

2. Underline the sentences that support the main idea.

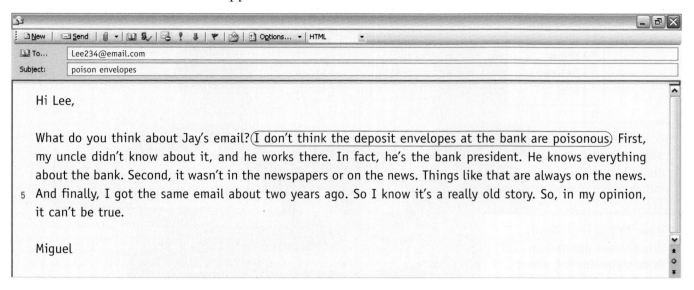

Hi Lee,

What do you think about Jay's email? (I don't think the deposit envelopes at the bank are poisonous.) First, my uncle didn't know about it, and he works there. In fact, he's the bank president. He knows everything about the bank. Second, it wasn't in the newspapers or on the news. Things like that are always on the news.
5 And finally, I got the same email about two years ago. So I know it's a really old story. So, in my opinion, it can't be true.

Miguel

B ▶ **Write it.** Write a paragraph about an urban legend.

1. Choose three urban legends from this unit. Complete the chart below.

Urban Legend	Do you believe it? *Yes* or *No*.	Why? (Three reasons for your opinion)
1.		1. 2. 3.
2.		1. 2. 3.
3.		1. 2. 3.

2. Choose one urban legend from the chart. Write an email to someone about what you think of the legend and why. Write one paragraph.

3. Edit your paragraph.
- Does your topic sentence express your opinion?
- Do you include at least three reasons for your opinion?

A ▶ Read.

1. Underline the main idea.

Global Communication on the Internet

Global communication on the Internet has a lot of benefits. For example, anyone can use the Internet to find information from all over the world. People can take online classes, so
5 they can learn even if they can't go to school. And email is an inexpensive way for us to keep in touch with friends and family who are far away from us. But global communication on the Internet can also cause problems.
10 If you have an email address, you probably get spam. Spam is email from people you don't know. These people try to sell you things. Many people waste a lot of time deleting spam from their email inboxes. But spam is not just a waste of time. People can use spam to get your personal information. This is called
15 "phishing." If "phishers" get your personal information, they can use your credit cards, take money from your bank account, and get new credit cards with your name on them. Also, sometimes emails contain viruses. Viruses can damage your computer and make it very slow. Viruses can also destroy all of your data, such
20 as music, documents, and pictures. So global communication can make your life easier, but you have to be careful.

2. Checkpoint. Answer these questions with a partner.

1. What is the writer's opinion about global communication on the Internet?

2. What are some benefits of global communication on the Internet?

3. What problems can global communication on the Internet cause?

B ▶ Listen.

1. Listen to the story.
What problem is the speaker talking about? _____

2. Checkpoint. Answer these questions.

1. What happened to the speaker? _____

_____

2. What lesson did the speaker learn? _____

C ▶ Wrap it up.

1. [TOEFL® iBT] The speaker's story in the listening section _____ the writer's opinion.

a. makes an inference about   c. supports
b. asks about   d. contrasts

2. What example does the speaker give? _____

3. What do you do when you get email from people you don't know? How do you protect your computer from viruses? _____

_____

Answers to Activity C, page 79: 1. hoax; 2. hoax; 3. true

Expansion Units 7–9

LISTENING AND CONVERSATION

A ▶ **Warm up.**

1. Read about each hotel. Then write the letter of each hotel under the correct photo.

1. _____   2. _____   3. _____   4. _____

A. Beverly Wilshire Hotel in Beverly Hills

• near Los Angeles

• Total number of rooms: 398

• Average nightly cost for a double room: $500
Located in the center of Beverly Hills. Perfect
place for business travelers and for tourists.
Full busines center; heated outdoor pool. Lots
of fine shops and restaurants just outside
the door.

C. The Standard in West Hollywood

• near Los Angeles

• Total number of rooms: 139

• Average nightly cost for a double room: $175
Cool hotel with a 1960s interior design. Disk
jockey booth in the lobby and a pool and
nightclub on the roof. Rooms come in six
different sizes. Walking distance to many
award-winning restaurants.

B. Mayfair Hotel

• downtown Los Angeles

• Total number of rooms: 291

• Average nightly cost for a double room: $85
Historic hotel is just eight blocks from the
convention center. Offers free wireless
Internet service, a small fitness room, a
restaurant, and meeting rooms.

D. Westin Bonaventure Hotel

• downtown Los Angeles

• Total number of rooms: 1,354

• Average nightly cost for a double room: $199
LA's largest hotel. Next to the convention
center. Hotel complex has 42 restaurants and
shops. Just minutes away from Universal
Studios, Disneyland, Beverly Hills, and
Hollywood. Every room offers fantastic
city views.

2. Answer these questions with a partner.

Which hotel ......

1. is the biggest? _____

2. is the smallest? _____

3. is the cheapest? _____

4. is the most expensive? _____

5. is probably the quietest? _____

6. is probably the most modern? _____

7. is probably the most unusual? _____

8. do you like the best? Why? _____

🎧 **B ▶ Listen.** Listen to the three phone messages on Susan's answering machine. Check (✓) the hotel Susan will recommend for each caller.

	The Beverly Wilshire	The Mayfair	The Standard	The Westin
Carol	☐	☐	☐	☐
George	☐	☐	☐	☐
Charlie	☐	☐	☐	☐

C ▶ Pair work. What was the tone of voice of each speaker? Discuss these questions with a partner.

1. Which speaker was enthusiastic? _____

2. Which speaker was stressed out? _____

3. Which speaker was tired? _____

🎧 **D ▶ Listen again.**

1. Listen for details to support your choices in Activity B. Write notes in the chart in Activity B.

2. Discuss your choices and supporting details with a partner.

Example:

A: I think that the _____ is the best hotel for Carol. She needs _____ .

B: In my opinion, the _____ is the best hotel for Carol. She _____ .

E ▶ Survey.

1. In your opinion, what are the most important factors in choosing a hotel? Rank the hotel factors from 1 (the most important) to 8 (the least important).

____ cost   ____ gym or fitness room

____ location   ____ free Internet service

____ pool   ____ size of hotel

____ safety   ____ size of rooms

2. In small groups, compare your rankings. What is the most important factor to most people? What factor most often ranked last? Then share your answers with the class.

A ▶ **Vocabulary boost!** For each **bold** word, choose the best definition.

1. Melbourne, Australia is a very **livable** city.
   a. alive; not dead   b. easy to live in

2. The **climate** in Melbourne is not too hot. The average summer temperature is 28° Celsius (82.4° Fahrenheit).
   a. weather conditions   b. summer temperature

3. There is a lot of **culture** in the city of Melbourne. You can see some kind of entertainment or visit a museum there every day.
   a. art, music, dance, theater   b. museums

4. There are many intelligent, **sophisticated** people in that busy city.
   a. worldly; educated   b. crowded

5. Many tourists visit the **art galleries**.
   a. places to make art   b. places to buy art

6. **Residents** of Melbourne are proud of their city.
   a. people who live in a place   b. people who visit a city

> **TIP** **Getting Meaning from Context**
> Remember that you can look in surrounding sentences to help guess the meaning of a word. You can also look at parts of a word to help you understand the meaning.

B ▶ **Read.** Scan the reading and underline the six words from Activity A. Read the sentence that each word is in. Do you need to change any of your answers in Activity A?

The World's Most Livable City

What makes a city the most livable in the world? According to an organization called the Economic Intelligence Unit (EIU) in London, England, there are 12 factors, including climate, culture and entertainment, transportation, housing, jobs, and safety. Every year the EIU surveys 130 cities around the world to figure out which city is the most livable.

5   Recently, the EIU ranked Melbourne, Australia, as the best city in the world to call home. Melbourne is a very sophisticated city, with lots of art galleries, trendy shops, and a wide variety of restaurants. People in
10 Melbourne enjoy mild weather—not too hot and not too cold. Melbourne offers many opportunities to watch sporting events, as well as cultural events such as plays, concerts, and festivals. Residents of Melbourne can
15 enjoy living in a safe and clean city. No wonder this city ranks number one in the world.

C ▶ Discuss.

1. What organization ranked Melbourne the most livable city in the world?
2. In your opinion, what other cities are very livable?
3. What about your city or town? What are some good things about it?

D ▶ Read again. Answer these questions.

1. The EIU ranked cities according to 12 factors. What seven factors are mentioned in the article?

   _____

   _____

2. What other factors could be used to rank a city? _____

3. In your opinion, what makes a city livable? Which factor is the most important about a city?

   _____

   _____

E ▶ Write about it. Write a paragraph about a city or town that you like.

1. Think about these questions. Then write your ideas in the mind map.
   - What's the name of the city?
   - Why is this city a good place to live? Give three reasons.
   - For each reason, give one example.

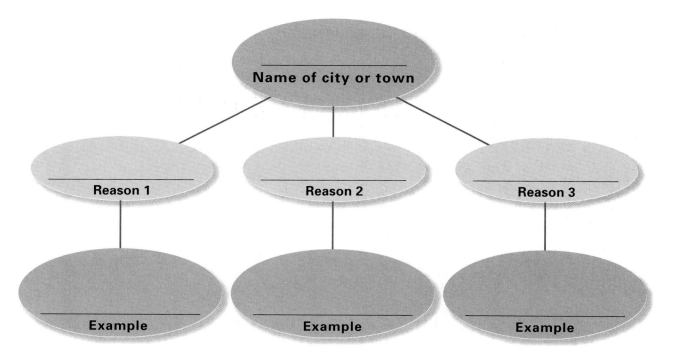

2. Write your paragraph. Use information from the graphic organizer above.

3. Edit your paragraph.
   - Circle the main idea. Underline the examples that support the main idea.
   - Do your examples support your opinion about the city or town?

READING AND SPEAKING

A ▶ Warm up. Do you want to take a vacation in outer space? Why or why not? Where do you want to go?

∩ B ▶ Read. Scan the article quickly. Find the answers to the questions below. Circle a, b, or c.

1. What is the name of Branson's space travel company?
   a. Virgin Galactic
   b. Virgin Atlantic
   c. Space Tours

2. How much is Richard Branson's company going to charge for a flight to space?
   a. about $2,000
   b. about $200,000
   c. about $2,000,000

SPACE TOURISM: IT'S OUT OF THIS WORLD!

Where did you take your last vacation? Did you travel by car, train, or plane? Did your hotel have a nice view? Well, in a few years, you might be able to take a vacation
5 in **outer space**! Several people, including Richard Branson, are working to get tourists into space. Branson is a multimillionaire **businessman** and **daredevil**. He's best known for his Virgin brand, which includes megastores and **airlines**. And he once tried to fly around the world in a **hot-air balloon**.
Branson is co-owner of the Spaceship Company. It's going to build **spaceships** that can carry seven passengers
10 and two **crew members**. Branson's **space travel** company, Virgin Galactic, is going to start offering passenger flights in just a few years. The spaceships will fly over 80 miles (130 kilometers) away from Earth. That's six times higher than regular airplanes fly. The cost for a seat on a Virgin Galactic flight is going to be about $200,000.
Of course, space tourists are probably going to want to spend a little time in space after their long flights. Even
15 now, companies are designing space hotels. Just think, a few years from now you could be spending your vacation orbiting the Earth and enjoying an up-close view of the stars from your floating hotel!

C ▶ Read again. Check (✓) *Q* for *Quote* or *P* for *Paraphrase* for each sentence. Then paraphrase the direct quotes on a separate piece of paper.

Sentences	Q	P
1. Branson's new company is going to build spacecrafts that will hold a small number of passengers and crew.	☐	☐
2. Branson's space travel company, Virgin Galactic, is going to start offering passenger flights in just a few years.	☐	☐
3. Branson's spaceships will reach a height of about 80 miles, which is about six times higher than an airplane can fly.	☐	☐
4. The cost for a seat on a Virgin Galactic flight is going to be about $200,000.	☐	☐

Skill Focus **Paraphrasing**
When you paraphrase something, you say or write the same thing in a different way. Read the passage you want to paraphrase and think about what it means. Then write the main ideas and details using your own words. For example:

Quote: "Several people, including Richard Branson, are working to get tourists into space."

Paraphrase: Richard Branson and others want to offer tours of space soon.

D ▶ Discuss. Ask and answer these questions with a partner.

1. What are three reasons people might want to vacation in space?
2. Do you think space travel is a good idea? Why or why not?

VOCABULARY Compound Nouns

A ▶ Identify. Write each noun in the correct column in the chart.

| airline | crew members | hot-air balloon | space travel |
| businessman | daredevil | outer space | spaceship |

Closed Compound Nouns	Open and Hyphenated Compound Nouns
airline	

B ▶ Pair work. Complete these sentences with seven words from Activity A. Then discuss the questions with a partner.

1. Richard Branson is a successful _____ and he is co-owner of a space travel company. What world-famous brand is he well known for?

2. Branson is a _____. What dangerous or risky thing did he do?

3. Virgin Galactic is going to build a _____ that can carry several passengers and a couple of _____. When will the company start offering flights?

4. Do you fly often? What's your favorite _____?

5. What do you think of _____? Do you want to fly around in _____?

Be going to for Future Plans

We use *be going to* with the base form of a verb to talk about the future.
> **I'm going to take** a vacation next month.
> Jack **isn't going to go** with me.

We can ask yes/no questions about the future.
> **Is** Anne **going to stay** at home this summer?

We can ask wh- questions about the future.
> Where **are** you **going to go** on Friday?

We use these expressions to talk about the future:
> *tonight, tomorrow, next week, in two weeks, on Friday, next month,*
> *next year, this weekend, this summer, in a few years, in the future, soon*

A ▶ **Practice.** Complete each sentence with the correct form of *be going to* and the words in parentheses.

1. Richard Branson (take) _____ people into space soon.

2. I think a lot of people (fly) _____ on Branson's spaceships in a few years.

3. I (go, not) _____ into space! I think it's crazy!

4. I (do, not) _____ anything this summer.

5. (you, travel) _____ on a Virgin Galactic space flight in the future?

6. Who (she, visit) _____ this summer?

🎧 B ▶ **Listen and read.** Listen to the conversation between May and Lin. Then read the paragraph below and circle the correct answers.

Lin and May are talking about vacations. Lin (is going to / isn't going to) go on vacation this
month. She (is going to / isn't going to) fly to Florida next month. Lin (is going to / isn't going to)
visit her friends in Florida; she's going to visit her family. May
says, "Mike and I (are going to / aren't going to) take a trip to
Mexico in June." May and Mike (are going to / aren't going to)
go to Costa Rica. Mike's brother James (is going to / isn't going
to) meet them in Mexico. Their vacations sound like fun.

ACTIVATING GRAMMAR

∩ A ▸ Listen and write.

1. Listen to the report. Read the items in the chart. Check (✓) Past or Future for each item.

	Past	Future
1. first space tourist	☐	☐
2. Barron Hilton's paper about space tourism	☐	☐
3. companies researching the cost of space travel	☐	☐
4. SpaceShipOne's flight 69 miles above Earth	☐	☐
5. Interorbital Systems's seven-day space vacations	☐	☐
6. Starchaser's three-passenger spaceship	☐	☐
7. Starchaser's 40-foot rocket	☐	☐
8. average people touring space	☐	☐

2. Answer the questions using *going to*. For yes/no questions, start the answer with *Yes* or *No*. Listen again to check your answers.

1. When is the average person going to vacation in space?

_____

2. Is Barron Hilton going to build a spaceship?

_____

3. What kind of vacations are people going to take with Interorbital Systems?

_____

4. What is the company Starchaser going to do?

_____

_____

5. Why do the people at Starchaser think it's important to get young people interested in space travel?

_____

_____

B ▸ Write and talk.
Write five sentences about what you are going to do next week—three true and two false. Read your sentences to a partner and have him or her guess which are true and which are false. Your partner should ask you questions to find out more.

Example: A: I'm going to study for a test next week.
        B: I think that's true. Are you going to study in the library or at home?

1. _____

2. _____

3. _____

4. _____

5. _____

A ▶ Discuss. Look at the two hotels and read the list of activities. Predict which things you can do at each hotel. Write *G* for Galaxy Orbit Hotel, *M* for Mountain View Lodge, or *G/M* for both. Discuss your answers with the class.

1. _____ hike
2. _____ look at the stars
3. _____ go to a museum
4. _____ bike
5. _____ ski

6. _____ shop
7. _____ get massages
8. _____ ride horses
9. _____ swim
10. _____ eat good food

∩ B ▶ Listen. Check (✓) the things that Trisha and Ed are going to do on their vacations.

1. _____ hike
2. _____ look at the stars
3. _____ go to a museum
4. _____ bike
5. _____ ski

6. _____ shop
7. _____ get massages
8. _____ ride horses
9. _____ swim
10. _____ eat good food

∩ C ▶ Listen again. Write the checked items from Activity B in the correct place in the Venn diagram to compare and contrast the two hotels. What can you do at each place? What can you do at both places?

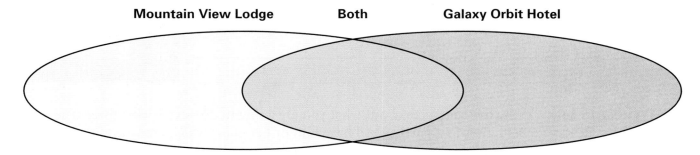

Mountain View Lodge   Both   Galaxy Orbit Hotel

D ▶ Pair work.

1. Circle the activities that you like to do. Then rank the eight from 1 (what you like the most) to 8 (what you like the least).

____ camp   ____ see movies   ____ sleep late   ____ ski

____ sunbathe   ____ take tours   ____ take walks   ____ ride horses

2. What do you like to do on your vacation? Tell your partner six things. Then make a Venn diagram comparing the things you and your partner like to do. Describe the similarities to the class.

∩ **A ▶ Listen and practice.** Then practice again using the other phrases.

A: Can you recommend a good restaurant near the hotel?

* Do you know a good . . .?
* Is there a good . . .?
* What's the best . . .?

A: Do we need reservations?

A: That's great! Thank you.

B: I suggest that you try Michael's Seafood. It's just down the street.

* I recommend . . .
* There's . . .
* I like . . .

B: No, you can just walk in.

B ▶ Pair work. Continue these conversations with a partner. Use the phrases from Activity A to ask for or give a recommendation.

1. **A:** Thanks. That was a great tour.
   B: You're welcome. What are you going to do now?
   A: Well, I'm really hungry. I'm in the mood for sushi.
   B: . . .

2. **A:** Excuse me, do you work here?
   B: Yes, I do. Can I help you with something?
   A: Well, I need to buy _____.

3. **A:** Hi, are you lost?
   B: Sort of. There are so many beaches here. We don't know which beach to go to.
   A: . . .

C ▶ Interview. Ask your classmates for recommendations. Complete the chart. Get three recommendations for each item.

	Recommendations
1. Restaurant	1. 2. 3.
2. Clothing store	1. 2. 3.
3. Coffee shop	1. 2. 3.
4. Other:	1. 2. 3.

A ▶ Study it. Read the brochure and the postcard. Underline the details in the brochure that are mentioned in the postcard. Circle the same details in the postcard. The first detail is done for you.

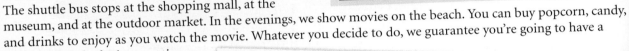

Sunset Beach: We have it all!

At Sunset Beach, you can do almost anything you want. You can <u>sunbathe</u> on our beautiful white sandy beaches. Have a delicious breakfast or lunch at our beachside café. You can also swim in the ocean next to dolphins and
5 turtles. The water is always warm and full of sea life. We provide towels, chairs, umbrellas, and sunscreen to all our guests. For people who like to start their days with a little exercise, we have a gym in the hotel with lots of equipment, and we offer yoga classes.
10   If you want to go into town, you can take our free shuttle bus. It goes into town once every hour. The shuttle bus stops at the shopping mall, at the museum, and at the outdoor market. In the evenings, we show movies on the beach. You can buy popcorn, candy, and drinks to enjoy as you watch the movie. Whatever you decide to do, we guarantee you're going to have a
15 wonderful and relaxing vacation.

Dear Teresa,

I'm so excited about my vacation at Sunset Beach! There's so much you can do, and I'm going to do
20 ALL of it. I'm going to spend my whole day at the beach. I'm going to (sunbathe) and swim with dolphins and turtles! And I'm going to eat breakfast and lunch right on the
25 beach, too! They have all of the beach gear you need—chairs, towels, umbrellas, and sunscreen. I'm also going to exercise in the gym and take yoga classes.

Teresa Jupa
1472 Lynn Lane
Austin, TX 73301

Greetings from
Sunset Beach

B ▶ Write it. Finish the postcard to Teresa. Paraphrase the rest of the brochure for Sunset Beach.

1. Imagine that you want to tell Teresa about the things you are going to do in the town near Sunset Beach. Underline those important details in the second half of the brochure.

2. Using the details you underlined, paraphrase the second half of the brochure in one paragraph and finish the postcard. Remember to use your own words.

3. Edit your paragraph.

   • Does your paragraph include all of the important ideas you underlined?

   • Does your paragraph include any ideas that do not describe what you are going to do in town? If it does, cross out these parts.

A ▶ Read.

1. Read the paragraph and underline the main idea.

People involved in developing space tourism believe that it can benefit society in several ways. First, space tourism may create thousands of new jobs. Space tourism companies will need pilots, mechanics, and many other employees. That is good for the economy. Second, outer space is still a

5 mystery. Space tourism can help us understand our world and our universe better. Private space tourism companies have a lot of money, and they can spend it on research. And finally, some people believe that we might have to live in outer space someday. But we don't know what will happen to our bodies after long periods of time in space. Space tourism can show us the

10 effects that space has on our bodies.

2. Checkpoint. Write the answers to these questions.

1. What is the writer's opinion about space tourism? _____

2. How many different reasons does the writer give to support this opinion? _____

3. What reasons does the writer give for his or her opinion? _____

B ▶ Listen.

1. What is the speaker's opinion about space tourism? _____

2. Checkpoint. Answer the questions with a partner

1. How many different reasons does the speaker give to support his opinion?
2. What reasons does the speaker give for his opinion?
3. Name two things that happen to astronauts' bodies when they go into outer space

C ▶ Wrap it up.

1. TOEFL® iBT The reading supports space tourism. What does the listening do?

    a. gives examples of space tourism   c. supports space tourism

    b. doesn't support space tourism   d. describes life in outer space

2. Discuss the reading and the listening with a partner. List the writer's supporting details on one side of the chart below and the speaker's details on the other side.

WRITER'S DETAILS (PROS)	SPEAKER'S DETAILS (CONS)

3. Which argument do you think is stronger? Why?

11

The Power of the Mind

READING AND SPEAKING

A ▶ Warm up. How much do these things hurt? Rank them in order from 1 (hurts a little) to 6 (hurts a lot).

1. ____ getting a paper cut

2. ____ breaking your leg

3. ____ burning your finger on the stove

4. ____ stepping on a piece of glass

5. ____ hitting your elbow on a table

6. ____ having a pebble in your shoe

B ▶ Read. Read the title and skim the article. What is the topic of the article? Circle a, b, c, or d.

a. new pain medications

b. differences between moderate and severe pain

c. how our thoughts affect pain

d. volunteers' experiences with heat

Pain: Do We Have to Feel It?

Late one night, you walk into the kitchen in your bare feet and step on something sharp. You're surprised to find a piece of glass stuck in your foot. It doesn't hurt much, but then your foot starts to bleed. As you begin to understand what's happening, the pain **increases**. Why?

The Study

5   Scientists at Wake Forest University School of Medicine wanted to understand how pain works. So they decided to do a study about pain and the brain. Volunteers in the study wore heating **devices** on their legs. The devices gave off different amounts of heat. The volunteers expected to feel **weak** heat seven seconds after a **signal**, **moderate** heat 15 seconds after, or **severe** heat 30 seconds
10 after. During the actual study, they sometimes received more or less heat than they expected. For example, they sometimes received severe heat after seven seconds. In these cases, volunteers said they felt less pain than they did when they received the same severe heat 30 seconds after the signal.

The Conclusions of the Study

15   The scientists found that our **expectations** play a role in the amount of pain we feel. When we feel pain, a **particular** part of the brain is active. The same part of the brain becomes active when we expect to feel pain. Think about this the next time you make an appointment to see your doctor. Will you believe it when your doctor has a needle in her hand and says, "This won't hurt a bit"?

C ▶ Read again. Choose the best alternative headings for paragraphs 2 and 3.

1. Paragraph 2:
   a. Volunteers for the Study
   b. Researching Pain and the Brain
   c. Heating Devices and Scientific Research

2. Paragraph 3:
   a. Believe Your Doctor
   b. Our Active Brains
   c. The Link between Expectations and Pain

> **Skill Focus** **Using Headings to Aid Comprehension**
> Headings are phrases placed before paragraphs in a reading. They identify the topic or main idea of the paragraph. We can preview the headings to help us think about the topic before we read.

D ▶ Discuss. Ask and answer the questions with a partner.

1. Would you volunteer to be in a study like the one in the reading? Why or why not?
2. Now you know that our expectations can control how much pain we feel. How can you use this information in your life?
3. Do you think your expectations control anything else in your life? Explain.

▼ VOCABULARY

A ▶ Identify. Match the words from the article with their definitions.

1. _____ increases   **a.** very strong
2. _____ device   **b.** a sound or movement that gives information
3. _____ signal   **c.** certain; specific
4. _____ weak   **d.** makes or becomes bigger
5. _____ moderate   **e.** what you think will happen
6. _____ severe   **f.** not very strong
7. _____ particular   **g.** not very weak or strong, not very big or small, etc.
8. _____ expectations   **h.** a tool designed to do a special job

B ▶ Practice. Complete the sentences with the words from Activity A.

1. I have a terrible cold. I feel really _____ and tired.

2. I have a _____ headache. My head hurts so much that I can't open my eyes.

3. I'm feeling _____ pain in my leg. It hurts, but it doesn't hurt a lot.

4. I always see a _____ doctor at the clinic. Her name is Dr. Philips.

5. The pain in my foot _____ when it rains. So I have to take more pain medication in rainy weather.

6. A smoke detector is an important _____ for any home. It gives a _____ when there is a fire.

7. The test was different from my _____. It was easy, not difficult.

A smoke detector is important.

> ### Verb + *to* + verb (*like, need, want, have, decide, plan, expect, hope*)
>
> We use infinitives (*to* + verb) with the following verbs: *need, want, would like, decide, expect, hope, plan.* This is true for statements and questions in all tenses.
>
> Leah **needs to have** an operation.
> Scientists **wanted to understand** how pain works.
> His patient **does not like to take** any pain medication.
> What did Alan **decide to do**?
> Did you **expect to recover** quickly?
> When do you **hope to get out** of the hospital?
> When are you **planning to have** your surgery?

A ▶ Practice. Find and correct the errors. If a sentence has no errors, write *correct*.

1. Jack wants see the doctor on Monday.

   _____

2. Did Ken decided to have surgery?

   _____

3. When are you planning to coming home?

   _____

4. Lida expected come home Tuesday.

   _____

5. Matt needs to takes his medicine.

   _____

6. Do you like to go to the doctor?

   _____

B ▶ Write and role-play. Unscramble the sentences in the conversation below. Be careful—some of them are questions. Then role-play the conversation with a partner.

1. Mia: you / do / What / to / do / plan _____

   you / to / Did / decide / surgery / have _____

2. Sara: Yes, I did. But I'm scared.

   like / stay / I / don't / in the hospital / to _____

3. Mia: wait / want / you / to / Do _____

4. Sara: No, I don't think I can wait.

   have / need / I / now / to / surgery _____

5. Mia: do / When / to the hospital / go / expect / to / you _____

6. Sara: morning / I / there / to / want / on Monday / be _____

   come / on Wednesday / And / I / to / home / hope _____

🎧 **A ▶ Listen and write.**

1. Complete the chart. Check (✓) *Gavin* or *Lisa* or both for each item.

	Gavin	Lisa
1. Who expected to do well on the driving exam?	✓	☐
2. Who expected to do badly on the interview?	☐	☐
3. Who needs to study?	☐	☐
4. Who would like to see a movie tonight?	☐	☐
5. Who doesn't like to go dancing during the week?	☐	☐
6. Who wants to get to bed early?	☐	☐
7. Who decided to take a 7:00 a.m. class?	☐	☐

2. Write the missing questions and answers about Gavin and Lisa. Use complete sentences.

1. Question: How did Gavin expect to do on his driving exam?

Answer: _____

2. Q: _____

A: Lisa expected to do badly on her interview.

3. Q: What does Gavin want to do tonight?

A: _____

4. Q: _____

A: Yes, Lisa is planning to see the movie with Mark.

5. Q: _____

A: No, Gavin doesn't like to go dancing during the week.

6. Q: _____

A: Lisa would like to go to bed early because she has an early class in the morning.

STUDENT DRIVER

B ▶ Write and talk. Ask your partner the questions and write the answers. Write your own question for number four.

1. When you expect to do something well, what happens? _____

_____

2. What do you like to do in the evenings? _____

_____

3. What are you planning to do after class today? _____

_____

4. *Your question:* _____

_____

A ▶ Discuss. Number the pictures in the correct order to tell a story.

a. _____

b. _____

c. _____

☊ B ▶ Listen. Check (✓) the things that the speakers mention.

	Things the Speakers Mention	Order of Events
a. Mrs. Lowe felt stress and fear.	✓	_____
b. Mrs. Lowe has a broken leg.	☐	_____
c. Mrs. Lowe's muscles got stronger and she felt less pain.	☐	_____
d. The creation of cortisol increased.	☐	_____
e. Mrs. Lowe ate some sugar for extra energy.	☐	_____
f. The car weighs two thousand pounds.	☐	_____
g. Mrs. Lowe saw her son trapped under her car.	☐	1
h. Stress sent a message to Mrs. Lowe's brain.	☐	_____

☊ C ▶ Listen again. Put the checked sentences from the chart in the correct order from 1 to 5. Then go back and check your answers to Activity A.

D ▶ Pair work.

1. Complete the sentences about stress with words from the box.

chronic	exhaustion	insomnia	symptom	tense

1. A stomachache can be a _____ of mild stress. Another effect of stress is a headache.

2. If you feel stressed all the time, you have _____ stress.

3. Stress can make your muscles feel _____. A hot bath can make them loosen up.

4. Stress can lead to _____. Even if you sleep, you will still feel tired.

5. Some stressed-out people have _____. They don't sleep for days.

2. On a chart like this, write four things about you and stress. Discuss them with a partner.

Things That Cause You Stress	Kinds of Stress They Cause	Ways to Make These Things Less Stressful
1. working all day at the computer	body stress, tight shoulders	stretch, take a short break every 30 minutes

∩ **A** ▶ **Listen and practice.** Then practice again using the other words and phrases.

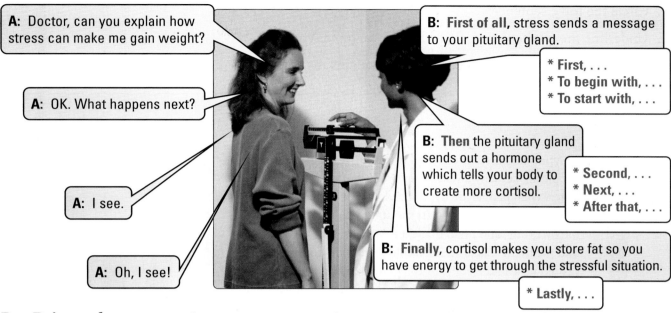

A: Doctor, can you explain how stress can make me gain weight?

A: OK. What happens next?

A: I see.

A: Oh, I see!

B: First of all, stress sends a message to your pituitary gland.

* First, . . .
* To begin with, . . .
* To start with, . . .

B: Then the pituitary gland sends out a hormone which tells your body to create more cortisol.

* Second, . . .
* Next, . . .
* After that, . . .

B: Finally, cortisol makes you store fat so you have energy to get through the stressful situation.

* Lastly, . . .

B ▶ **Pair work.** Continue these conversations with a partner. Use the words and phrases from Activity A to explain a process.

1. **A:** I get so stressed out at work.
   B: So do I. But I have a process for relaxing after a long day at work.
   A: Really? What do you do?
   B: Well, to begin with, . . . (Ideas: *take a long walk, sit quietly with my eyes closed for 15 minutes, make a nice dinner*)

2. **A:** This is delicious. What is it? How did you make it?
   B: It's _____. Well, first I . . .

3. **A:** Is this the registrar's office?
   B: Yes, it is. How can I help you?
   A: Can you tell me how to register for classes?
   B: . . .

C ▶ **Role-play.** Role-play conversations about the following topics. Be sure to use expressions to explain a process in your conversations. Check (✓) each expression after you hear it.

Topics
how to send email   how to make your favorite food
how to relax   *your idea*: _____

Phrases to Start Explaining a Process	Phrases to Continue Explaining a Process	Phrases to Finish Explaining a Process
First	Second	Finally
First of all	Next	Lastly
To begin with	Then	
To start with	After that	

A ▶ **Study it.** Read the article.

1. Circle the topic sentence.

2. Underline the two sentences that support the topic sentence.

3. What experience did the writer have that explains the second detail?

_____

   Hypnotism is so interesting! It is like sleep, but hypnotized people are actually awake. They are just in a very relaxed state. When people are hypnotized, they may believe what someone else tells them. Last month, I was hypnotized for
5 the first time, and I had that experience. When the hypnotist told me that I was drinking a cold drink, I told him that I could taste and feel the drink going down my throat. And when the hypnotist suggested that it was hot, I got warm and began to sweat. Do you want to be hypnotized?

B ▶ **Write it.** Write a paragraph about mind over matter.

1. Have you ever experienced a physical reaction to something you saw or heard, such as a movie or bad news? Write an experience on the left. Write two or three details about the experience on the right.

Experience	Details
1.	1.
	2.
	3.

2. Write a paragraph about a time that you had a physical reaction to something you saw or heard. Include a topic sentence (a sentence describing your experience) and two or three sentences about the experience.

3. Edit your paragraph.
   - Do you have a topic sentence?
   - Do you include two or three details about the experience?

A ▶ Read.

1. Read the paragraph. What problem does Mack have?

My name is Mack. I started college this year. It's a lot more challenging than I expected! I took five classes last semester, and I had to study all the time. I stayed up late every night
5 to study. I was always tired in the mornings, so I drank a lot of coffee. That really helped me stay awake during the day. I drank seven or eight cups of coffee every day. I studied all night before each final exam. I didn't even take
10 any breaks! I studied for five or six hours in a row. But I didn't get good grades. I'm so stressed out! I want to do better, but I don't know what to do!

2. Checkpoint. Answer the questions.

    1. Why was Mack so busy last semester? _____

    2. When did Mack study for his exams? _____

B ▶ Listen.

1. What is the speaker talking about? _____

2. Checkpoint. Answer the questions.

    1. What study tips does the speaker give? _____

    2. Why is it important to get a good night's sleep before taking a test? _____

    _____

C ▶ Wrap it up.

1. (TOEFL® iBT) Based on the listening, make an inference about what Mack can do to improve his test grades.

    a. Drink less coffee.   c.   Study harder.

    b. Don't study all night before an exam.   d.   Take fewer classes.

2. When do you study?

3. Do you take breaks while you are studying? If yes, what do you do during your breaks? If no, why not?

4. How can information in the listening affect your life? Now that you know this information, will you make any changes in your life?

12

Success Starts Early

READING AND SPEAKING

A ▸ Warm up. Discuss these questions with a partner.

1. When you were a child, what did you want to be when you grew up? Why?

2. Are you still interested in the same career, or do you have a different goal now? What kinds of things are you doing to achieve your goal?

B ▸ Read. Skim the article. Find the answers to the questions below.

1. Who is this reading about? _____

2. What is the writer's point of view, or opinion, of these people?
   Circle a, b, or c.
   a. She is impressed.
   b. She is not impressed.
   c. She is disappointed.

> **Skill Focus** **Understanding Point of View**
> A writer often has a reason for writing or an opinion about the topic he or she is writing about. This is called a point of view. A writer's point of view may be stated directly, or we may have to infer the writer's opinion based on what he or she writes.

Kevin Baillie and Ryan Tudhope's story is like a fairy tale. They have been friends since kindergarten. In high school, **independent,** talkative, **outgoing** Baillie wanted to be a lawyer. The **intelligent, quiet, thoughtful** Tudhope wanted to be an engineer or a scientist. But luckily for us, their plans changed one day in
5 the ninth grade, when they discovered a software program called 3D Studio.
They played around with the program for hours after school every day. After a while, they were able to make short movies. Someone liked one of the movies so much that he paid the boys $15,000 to create an advertisement for Seattle's Space Needle. Their excellent work on the advertisement got them jobs at
10 Microsoft when they were still only high school juniors! Then George Lucas heard about them. Only a week after they graduated from high school, they started working for him on *Star Wars: Episode 1.*
Now, the **capable** and **motivated** friends are visual effects supervisors at a top visual effects studio in San Francisco, California. The company, The Orphanage,
15 specializes in visual effects for movies and commercials. Including their time at The Orphanage (which began in 1999), they have worked together for about 15 years. They have worked on about 20 movies, including *Sin City, Harry Potter and the Goblet of Fire, Charlie's Angels 2,* and *Superman Returns.* These two **talented** young men have accomplished a lot in less than 30 years. Just imagine
20 what they'll do over the next 30 years!

C ▶ Read again. Read the excerpts below from the article. Which statements show that the writer is impressed by Baillie and Tudhope? Check (✔) them. Underline the words that tell you that the writer is impressed.

Words, Phrases, and Sentences

1. Kevin Baillie and Ryan Tudhope's story is <u>like a fairy tale.</u> ✔
2. Baillie wanted to be a lawyer.
3. Luckily for us, their plans changed one day in the ninth grade.
4. They were able to make short movies.
5. He paid the boys $15,000 to create an advertisement.
6. They have worked on about 20 movies.
7. These two talented young men have accomplished a lot in less than 30 years.
8. Just imagine what they'll do over the next 30 years!

D ▶ Discuss. Ask and answer these questions with a partner.

1. Why did Kevin Baillie and Ryan Tudhope start making movies?
2. Were Kevin and Ryan just lucky or very skillful?
3. Which is more important, luck or skill?

VOCABULARY Antonyms

A ▶ Identify. Match each adjective in column A to its opposite in column B.

A	B
1. ___ independent	a. unable
2. ___ outgoing	b. unskilled
3. ___ intelligent	c. shy
4. ___ quiet	d. lazy
5. ___ thoughtful	e. thoughtless
6. ___ capable	f. not smart
7. ___ motivated	g. needy
8. ___ talented	h. talkative

B ▶ Pair work. Work with a partner. Describe a person who fits an adjective in Activity A. Your partner will guess the adjective that describes that person.

Example: A: This person gets good grades, and she is very smart.
  B: She's intelligent!

The Present Perfect

We use the present perfect for actions that began in the past and continue in the present. Use *for* with amounts of time and *since* with dates and specific times.

> **A: Has** Ryan **known** Kevin **for** a long time?
> **B:** Yes, he **has known** Kevin **for** many years. (He still knows Kevin.)
> **A:** How long **has** Ryan **known** Kevin?
> He **has known** Kevin **since** 1983.
> He **has known** Kevin **since** kindergarten.
> **A:** Where **have** they **worked for** the last few years?
> **B:** They **'ve worked** at The Orphanage in San Francisco **for** a few years.

To form the present perfect, use the simple present of *have* with a past participle. To form past participles, add *–ed* to most verbs. To form the negative, place *not* between the verb *have* and the past participle. See page 132 for a list of irregular verbs and their past participles.

> I **have not seen** a movie for three months.

Some Irregular Verbs and Their Past Participles

be – been	have – had	know – known
do – done	go – gone	take – taken

A ▶ Practice. Complete each sentence with the present perfect of the verb in parentheses.

1. (be) _____ Joanna and Brian _____ here in Seattle for over a year?

2. Joanna (know) _____ Brian for five years.

3. Brian (do) _____ a lot in just a few years. He (finished) _____ school, and he (get) _____ a job.

4. Joanna (go) _____ back to Canada to visit her family three times since she moved here.

5. Joanna and I have some classes together. We (take, not) _____ any math classes since last year, but we're going to take calculus this semester.

B ▶ Read. Complete the dialogue with the present perfect of the verbs in parentheses and *for* or *since*.

A: I need to make some changes. I (do) _____₁_____ the same things _____₂_____ too long!

B: Really? Like what? How long (live) _____₃_____ here?

A: Well, I (be) _____₄_____ in this apartment _____₅_____ 2002 and in this city _____₆_____ I was born! I (go) _____₇_____ to the same gym _____₈_____ over five years.

B: Yeah, you (be) _____₉_____ at this gym _____₁₀_____ I started working here. It's a great gym!

A: Yeah, but I need to change something. Hmm. I (take, not) _____₁₁_____ a vacation _____₁₂_____ a couple of years. Maybe that's what I'll do—go to Buenos Aires! And if that's too expensive, I'll get a haircut. I (have) _____₁₃_____ the same style _____₁₄_____ I was 12.

B: Sure, start with your hair.

ACTIVATING GRAMMAR

⌂ A ▶ Listen and write.

1. Read the sentences about the conversation. The verbs in parentheses are in the present tense. Listen to the conversation and check (✓) the correct column for each sentence.

	Began and finished in the past	Began in the past and still true
1. Kim (wants) to be a singer.	☐	☐
2. She (sings) at her uncle's wedding.	☐	☐
3. She (is) in 22 talent competitions.	☐	☐
4. She (wins) a competition in Los Angeles.	☐	☐
5. She (is) successful since she recorded her first album.	☐	☐
6. Kim (has) two hit songs from her first album.	☐	☐
7. She (has) six more hit songs.	☐	☐
8. She (does) a lot of shows this year.	☐	☐

2. Rewrite each sentence from Activity 1 in the simple past or the present perfect.

1. _____
2. _____
3. _____
4. _____
5. _____
6. _____
7. _____
8. _____

> **TIP** ▶ Remember to use the simple past for actions that began and finished at a specific time in the past and the present perfect for actions that began in the past and continue in the present.

B ▶ Pair work.
Learn about a partner. Ask your partner the following questions. Answer in complete sentences.

1. Do you know any people who have won life-changing competitions? What did they win? How did their lives change?

2. Have you entered any contests or competitions? What kind? Did you win?

3. What job do you hope to do someday? What kinds of things have you already done that will help you get this kind of job in the future?

4. *Your question:* _____?

A ▶ Discuss. Look at the photos of Sondra Clark on the covers of her books. Check (✓) three things that you think are true about Sondra.

a. ____ She is very shy.

b. ____ She is young.

c. ____ She is talented.

d. ____ She is motivated.

e. ____ She is lazy.

f. ____ She is outgoing.

B ▶ Listen.

1. Listen to the information about Sondra Clark. Check (✓) True, False, or Information not given.

	True	False	Information Not Given
1. Clark has written a total of two books.	☐	☐	☐
2. Clark's mother is a writer.	☐	☐	☐
3. Clark's father is a writer.	☐	☐	☐
4. Clark went to Africa to sell her books.	☐	☐	☐
5. Clark has been to many different countries with Childcare International.	☐	☐	☐
6. Clark has raised a lot of money for people in need.	☐	☐	☐

C ▶ Listen again. Check (✓) the best summary of the report about Sondra Clark.

a. ____ Sondra Clark is a capable, independent, talented girl. She has raised thousands of dollars to help children around the world.

b. ____ Sondra Clark is a talented and intelligent girl. She writes books and raises money for organizations that help children in need.

c. ____ Sondra Clark is a young, talented, and motivated girl. She has written several books and has done a lot of work to help others.

D ▶ Pair work.

1. Think of a goal that you would like to accomplish. It can be a small goal, like passing a test, or a big goal, like writing a book or starting a career. On a piece of paper, describe your goal in two to four sentences.

2. Talk with a partner. Discuss your goals. Work together to write five steps toward achieving your goal.

A ▶ Listen and practice. Then practice again using the other questions and phrases.

A: I have a problem. I want to work with a visual effects company in San Francisco when I graduate, but I don't know what to study. **What do you think I should do?**

* **Do you have any advice?**
* **Do you have any suggestions?**
* **What do you recommend that I do?**

A: OK, thanks. I'll try it.

B: **I think you should** look at the company's website. Read their job descriptions to see what kinds of people they want to hire.

* **You might want to . . .**
* **If I were you, I would . . .**
* **You should probably . . .**

B: You're welcome. Good luck!

B ▶ Pair work. Continue these conversations with a partner. Use the questions and phrases from Activity A to ask for or give advice.

1. **A:** What are you doing?
   B: Well, I'm researching companies. I'd like to get a job after graduation, but I'm not sure what to do.

2. **A:** Hi! What's up?
   B: I have an interview for my dream job tomorrow. But I don't know what to wear! . . .

3. **A:** I have a problem. I _____.
   What _____?
   B: . . .

C ▶ Practice. Work with a partner to ask for and give advice about the following topics. Check (✓) each expression after you use or hear it.

Topics		
_____ you want to write a book	_____ you don't know what kind of career you want	_____ you want to learn something new
_____ you want to improve your English	_____ you can't fall asleep at night	_____ your idea: _____

Expressions to Ask for Advice	Expressions to Give Advice
_____ What do you think I should do?	_____ I think you should . . .
_____ Do you have any advice?	_____ You might want to . . .
_____ Do you have any suggestions?	_____ If I were you, I would . . .
_____ What do you recommend that I do?	_____ You should probably. . .

A ▶ Study it.   Read the journal entry. On the plan outline, write the steps that the writer took.

When I was in high school, I knew I wanted to go to
college, but my family didn't have much money.
However, I have always been a very stubborn person,
and I don't give up easily when I want something.
5   So I made a plan and worked really hard to achieve
my goal. The first step in my plan was to talk to
the college counselor at my school. She told me
about all of the different ways I could get money
for college. After I talked to her, I researched all of
10   the different loans, grants, and financial aid that
were available, and then I applied for every kind of aid
that I could find. Then I researched scholarships.
After getting that information, I applied for so many
different scholarships that I lost count. After I did
15   all of that, I got a part-time job. By the time I
graduated from high school, I had about $5,000 in
my savings account, and I had a loan, financial aid,
and four scholarships. It wasn't easy, but with a
little planning and a lot of hard work, I reached my
20   goal. I have been in college for three years now and
I love it!

Goal: Go to College
Plan Outline

Step 1: _____

_____

Step 2: _____

_____

Step 3: _____

_____

Step 4: _____

_____

Step 5: _____

_____

Step 6: _____

_____

B ▶ Write it.   Write a journal entry about a successful goal that you have achieved.

1. Think of something that you worked for and succeeded in achieving. What happened? What steps
did you take to reach your goal? Write the goal on the left and the steps that you took on the right.

Goal	Plan Outline: Steps
	1.
	2.
	3.
	4.

2. Write a journal entry about a goal that you achieved successfully. Include a topic sentence, a sentence
describing your goal, and three or four sentences describing the steps you took to successfully achieve
your goal.

3. Edit your journal entry. Then tell your story to a partner. To edit:
   • Underline the topic sentence.
   • Number the steps.

PUTTING IT TOGETHER

A ▸ Read.

1. Read the article and choose the best title. Circle a, b, or c.

    a. Clean, Safe Drinking Water for Everyone!
    b. A Small Boy Makes a Big Dream Come True
    c. Thousands Die Every Day from Drinking Dirty Water

Photograph provided by
Ryan's Well Foundation
www.ryanswell.ca

In 1998, Ryan Hreljac [pronounced HURL-jack] was six years old. One day at school, he learned that thousands of children die every day because they have only dirty water to drink. He was shocked by the news. So he decided to raise money for a well in an African village.

Ryan, a Canadian, did extra chores to earn money. He sometimes had to wash windows or clean the house while his brothers played outside. After a few months, he met his goal of raising $70. But he found out that he needed to raise $2,000 to build a well. It was difficult, but after a few months, Ryan raised enough money to build a well next to Angolo Primary School in Uganda.

After that experience, Ryan wanted to continue to raise money to build wells in developing countries. In 2001, he started an organization called Ryan's Well Foundation. Ryan is now a teenager and he has devoted his life to helping people around the world get clean, safe drinking water. Since 1998, Ryan has helped raise over 1.5 million dollars and has completed more than 250 water and sanitation projects. Ryan's story shows us that anyone, even a six-year-old boy, can find a way to make a dream come true.

2. Checkpoint. Write the answers to these questions.

    1. What was Ryan Hreljac's first goal? _____

    2. How did he achieve his first goal? _____

    3. Where was Ryan's first well? _____

    4. What can people learn from Ryan's experience? _____

B ▸ Listen.

1. Listen to the news report. Where is the reporter?

2. Checkpoint. Answer the questions with a partner.

    1. Where did villagers near the Angolo Primary School get their water before they got their well?
    2. What was wrong with this water?

C ▸ Wrap it up.

1. TOEFL® iBT The reading tells the story of Ryan Hreljac. What does the listening do?

    a. identifies pros and cons of his actions   c. summarizes the article
    b. expresses a point of view   d. identifies the effects of his actions

2. How did Ryan's actions affect the community in Uganda? Name three things.

3. Describe an experience when your actions caused something good or bad to happen to other people.

Expansion Units 10–12

LISTENING AND CONVERSATION A Cause for Celebration

A ▶ Warm up. Look at the photos of four celebrations. In small groups, answer these questions about each photo. (Answers will vary.)

1. Have you been to a similar celebration? Describe the last time you went to this type of celebration.

2. Do you plan to go to a similar celebration in the near future? Explain.

3. How are these photos similar to or different from celebrations in your culture?

In the U.S., graduates often throw their caps in the air at the end of the ceremony.

Guests throw rice on the wedding couple for good luck.

Birthday celebrations are often informal gatherings.

At midnight on New Year's Eve, people enjoy making a lot of noise.

B ▶ Listen. Check (✓) the best summary for the conversation.

1. _____ Emily and Tom are planning a surprise party for Emily's friend Patricia. They decide to have it at Emily's apartment. They are going to invite Patricia's family and some of her friends. Tom is going to bake the cake.

2. _____ Emily and Tom are planning a surprise party for Emily's friend Patricia. They decide to have it at Emily's apartment. Emily is going to invite Patricia over to see Emily's new couch. For the party, they are going to invite Patricia's family and some of her friends from the tennis team. Tom is a good baker, so he is going to bake the cake.

3. _____ Emily and Tom are planning a surprise party. Tom is going to bake the cake. Emily and Tom are good friends.

C ▶ Discuss. Discuss these questions with a partner. (Answers will vary.)

1. What are Emily and Tom planning?
2. Have you ever had a surprise party or been to a surprise party? Describe it.
3. Name five things that you think are important to create a good party.

∩ D ▶ Listen again. Then answer these questions.

1. How long has it been since Patricia was at Emily's apartment? _____

2. Why doesn't Emily want to invite a lot of people? _____

3. How is Emily going to get Patricia to come to her house? _____

4. How can you infer that Tom is good at baking? _____

E ▶ Group work.

1. Think of an event to celebrate. In small groups, ask for suggestions and recommendations. Use expressions in the chart. Use your imagination to plan the best possible celebration.

Asking for Recommendations	Giving Recommendations
Can you recommend...?	I think you should...
Can you help me...?	If I were you, I would...
	You should probably...
	I suggest that you try...

2. Answer the questions. Then write a description of the celebration you have planned. Share your description with your class.

1. What type of celebration are you going to have? _____

2. Where is it going to be? _____

3. Who are you going to invite? _____

4. What food are you going to serve? _____

5. What special things are you going to have at the celebration? _____

_____

3. Listen to your classmates' descriptions of celebrations. Write your opinion in the chart. Then take a vote and write the class's opinion in the chart.

	My Opinion	Class's Opinion
The Most Unusual		
The Most Expensive		
The Most Fun		

A ▶ Vocabulary boost! Scan the article to find these words. Circle each word and read the sentence it is in. Then choose the correct meaning. Circle a or b.

1. talented
   a. very good at something

   b. famous

2. unknown
   a. popular

   b. not known by other people

3. choir
   a. a music band

   b. a singing group

4. professional
   a. doing an activity for money

   b. doing an activity for free

5. encouraged
   a. became brave or confident

   b. helped someone become brave or confident

6. competition
   a. a singer

   b. a contest

7. turning point
   a. a time when everything stops

   b. a time of important change

⌂ B ▶ Read.

1. As you read the article, underline the main ideas about Kelly Clarkson's life. Underline the important things she did or things that happened.

Kelly Clarkson
From an Unknown to a Star

Have you ever dreamed of becoming a famous singer or movie star? Many talented, or good, singers dream about having a hit song, but few people actually reach that goal. Kelly Clarkson was an unknown singer and actress with such a dream. Clarkson
5 was born in Texas in 1982. She had a difficult childhood because she moved from place to place with her mother.

Singing was not Clarkson's only dream. When she was 11 years old, she wanted to become a marine biologist. But a teacher heard her singing and asked her to join the choir at school. She
10 loved to sing but had never had formal training. In high school, she continued to sing and perform.

After graduating from high school, Clarkson made a short CD of her singing, but no recording companies were interested in her. She decided to move to Hollywood, California, because
15 she wanted to become a professional singer or actress. After two years with little success, she moved back to Texas.

In 2002, her friends encouraged her to enter the new TV competition, American Idol. She entered the contest, along with 10,000 other hopeful singers. She was one of the 30
20 finalists. Her beautiful voice and talented performances helped her win the competition. Since that time, she has released two albums and has continued to be a popular and successful singer. Winning the contest was the turning point in her professional career. Since that contest, her life has never been the same.

2. When you paraphrase, you write something in your own words. Read the excerpt from the article. Then choose the better paraphrase. Discuss your answer with a partner.

> **Excerpt:** She decided to move to Hollywood, California, because she wanted to become a professional singer or actress. After two years with little success, she moved back to Texas.

    a. _____ She decided to move because she planned to be a singer or actress. After two years, she moved to Texas.

    b. _____ She went to Hollywood, California to become a singer or an actress. But after two unsuccessful years, she returned to Texas.

C ▶ Discuss. Discuss these questions in small groups.

    1. What was Clarkson's original dream as a child?

    2. Why do you think her goal changed? Who influenced her?

    3. Have you heard Kelly Clarkson's music? Who are some of your favorite singers?

D ▶ Read again. Choose the best heading for paragraphs 3 and 4.

    1. Paragraph 3:
        a. Clarkson Starts to Sing
        (b.) Clarkson Chases her Dream
        c. Clarkson Moves to Texas
    2. Paragraph 4:
        (a.) A Competition Changes Clarkson's Life
        b. Clarkson's Beautiful Voice
        c. Clarkson Enters a Competition

E ▶ Write about it. Follow these steps to write about a partner's life 10 years from now.

1. Pair work. Imagine that it is 10 years in the future. Your life has been like a dream—many wonderful things have happened and you have reached many goals. With a partner, describe your lives as you imagine them. Ask each other questions about your imagined lives. Ask your partner to describe the steps he or she has taken to achieve a particular goal.

2. On a piece of paper, identify the key steps that helped your partner reach one of his or her goals. Then use this list to write a paragraph about your partner, describing the sequence of events he or she took to reach the goal. Remember to use the simple past and present perfect.

3. Write your paragraph, but don't write your name or your partner's name on your paper. Be sure to add a title to your paragraph.

4. With your classmates, mix all of the papers together. Choose one paragraph to read. Can you guess who it is about?

VOCABULARY EXPANSION ACTIVITIES

A ▶ Practice. Complete the sentences with words from the box.

action movies	classical	comedies	favorite	hip-hop	horror movies

1. My _____ kind of food is spaghetti.

2. I love _____ because I like to laugh.

3. My brother really likes _____ because of the loud noises and fast pace.

4. _____ music is OK, but I think that it's too old for young people. Also, I'm not crazy about big orchestras with a lot of violins.

5. I like to dance to _____ music because it has a really modern beat and fantastic singing.

6. My little brother doesn't like to watch _____ because he gets too scared.

B ▶ Pair work. Write answers to these questions. Then discuss them with a partner.

1. What do you do in your free time? _____

    _____

2. What are your interests? _____

    _____

3. What is your favorite kind of music? _____

    _____

4. What is your favorite kind of food? What is your favorite drink? _____

    _____

5. Do you have a nickname? _____

    _____

6. What do you dislike? _____

    _____

7. What kind of movies do you like? _____

    _____

8. Do you have a pet? _____

    _____

A ▶ Practice. Complete the sentences with *get, take,* or *go*. Then check (✓) whether the sentence is true or false for you.

		True	False
1. I usually _____ a lot of sleep.		☐	☐
2. I never _____ night classes.		☐	☐
3. I never _____ stressed out.		☐	☐
4. I often _____ on a picnic.		☐	☐
5. I always _____ enough exercise.		☐	☐
6. I rarely _____ to the movies.		☐	☐
7. I sometimes _____ a vacation.		☐	☐
8. I never _____ vitamins.		☐	☐

B ▶ Pair work. Write about each of your answers in Activity A. Then discuss them with a partner. If a statement is true for you, offer more information.

Example: I rarely *go* to the movies, but I rent DVDs every week.

If a statement is false for you, change it to a true statement, and give more information.

Example: I never *get* enough exercise. I joined a gym, but I never go.

1. _____

_____

2. _____

_____

3. _____

_____

4. _____

_____

5. _____

_____

6. _____

_____

7. _____

_____

8. _____

_____

A ▶ **Multiple choice.** Circle the letter of the correct answer.

1. Where can you see exhibitions?
   a. in a theater
   b. in a museum
   c. in a restaurant

2. Where can you get on a train or streetcar?
   a. in a subway station
   b. in an amusement park
   c. in a theater

3. Where can you buy something to eat or drink?
   a. in banks, coffee shops, and subway stations
   b. in coffee shops, malls, and restaurants
   c. in gyms, banks, and clubs

4. Where can you see trees, statues, and fountains?
   a. in a park
   b. in a club
   c. in a museum

5. Where can you see a movie or a play?
   a. in a doctor's office
   b. in a subway station
   c. in a theater

B ▶ **Pair work.** Ask your partner the questions. Write his or her answers.

1. What restaurants do you like in your city? _____
   _____

2. Is there a subway in your city? Do you ever take it? _____
   _____

3. What is the best park in your city? Describe it. _____
   _____

4. Where do you go for entertainment? _____
   _____

5. What bank do you use? Are you happy with your bank? _____
   _____

6. Where do you go to get exercise? _____
   _____

7. Is there an amusement park near your home? What rides or attractions does it have? _____
   _____

8. Where do you like to go shopping in your city? _____
   _____

A ▶ What do you like to do? Rank the activities below. Write *1* next to the activity that you like best and *13* next to the activity you like least.

a. _____ going snowboarding

b. _____ eating at a restaurant

c. _____ sunbathing at the beach

d. _____ talking with friends

e. _____ going ice-skating

f. _____ going swimming

g. _____ having a picnic

h. _____ playing volleyball

i. _____ going skiing

j. _____ getting fresh air

k. _____ getting some exercise

l. _____ listening to the ocean

m. _____ relaxing in the sand

B ▶ Class discussion. Compare your answers to activity A with your classmates. Write answers to the questions below.

1. What are the class's favorite activities? _____

_____

_____

_____

2. What activities aren't popular? _____

_____

_____

_____

3. Do people in your class prefer to relax or to exercise? Explain. _____

_____

_____

_____

4. What places are popular for vacations? _____

_____

_____

_____

A ▶ Practice. Complete the sentences with words from the box.

boring	discover	exciting	hoax	fascinating	mysterious

1. Skiing is _____! Going down a mountain really fast is a little dangerous and my heart starts pumping quickly!

2. I'm not interested in Elvis Presley. I think that his music is _____.

3. This book about pyramids is _____. I'm really interested in Egyptian history.

4. I think that crop circles are very _____. No one really knows where they come from.

5. Crop circles are a _____! Some college students are tricking people.

6. I hope that scientists will _____ more secret doors in pyramids.

B ▶ Practice. Write two synonyms for each word.

1. discover   _____   _____

2. exciting   _____   _____

3. mysterious   _____   _____

4. hoax   _____   _____

C ▶ Group discussion. In small groups, write a noun that can be described by each adjective.

1. exciting: _____

2. mysterious: _____

3. fascinating: _____

4. strange: _____

5. boring: _____

A ▶ Multiple choice. Circle the letter of the expression that has the same meaning as the underlined words.

1. Sam <u>really likes</u> football.
   a. turns down
   b. is crazy about
   c. is here to stay

2. Extreme sports <u>are going to be popular for a long time</u>.
   a. are here to stay
   b. are worth every penny
   c. give people the creeps

3. This painting costs a lot, but <u>it's a good value for the money</u>.
   a. it's really taking off
   b. it costs an arm and a leg
   c. it's worth every penny

4. That horror movie really <u>scared me</u>!
   a. is taking off
   b. is here to stay
   c. gave me the creeps

5. One night at that hotel <u>is very expensive</u>.
   a. costs an arm and a leg
   b. is worth every penny
   c. is really taking off

6. That band really <u>became successful</u> last year.
   a. turned down
   b. took off
   c. was crazy about

7. He offered me $10,000 for my hair collection, but I <u>refused</u>.
   a. turned him down
   b. took off
   c. was worth every penny

A ▶ Practice. Complete the email with words from the box.

cell phone	keyboard	recharge	surf	website
displays	online	screen	text message	

To...   mary.smith@groover.com

Subject: Our new computer!

Mary,

Are you surprised to get an email from me? Your grandfather and I just bought a computer! We'll be able to keep in touch more easily now. It has a special _____ so that we can type easily. We

bought a computer with a very large _____ so that we can see everything. It

5 _____ words in a big size, which helps us read and write! We really like the Internet. We

_____ the web almost every day. We like to go _____ in the evenings

instead of watching TV. Our favorite _____ has news and weather.

We also bought a _____ so we can call our friends even when we're not at home. We don't

just talk, of course. Sometimes we send a _____. It's a little hard to type the words on

10 such a small area, but we're learning fast. Our only problem is that we use it a lot. Sometimes we forget to

_____ it and the battery goes dead.

We'll call you soon! We hope that you are well.

Love,

Grandma

A ▶ **Matching.** Match each word or phrase with its definition.

1. ____ ghost
2. ____ all the rage
3. ____ materials
4. ____ tent
5. ____ wear out
6. ____ made a fortune

a. became very rich
b. kinds of cloth, for example, cotton and wool
c. become useless
d. very popular
e. a shelter that is made of fabric
f. the spirit of a dead person

B ▶ **Group discussion.** Write answers to these questions. Then discuss them in small groups.

1. What is all the rage right now? _____

_____

_____

_____

2. Give an example of someone who made a fortune. _____

_____

_____

_____

3. What is your favorite material for clothing? _____

_____

_____

_____

4. Do you believe in ghosts? Why or why not? _____

_____

_____

_____

5. Have you slept in a tent? How did you like it? _____

_____

_____

_____

6. How often do you wear jeans? _____

_____

_____

_____

UNIT 7 Verbs with Sports and Activities

A ▶ Practice. Complete the sentences with *do, play, go,* or *X* if no word is necessary. Then check (✓) whether the sentence is true or false for you.

	True	False
1. I love to _____ surfing.	☐	☐
2. I never _____ jog.	☐	☐
3. I can _____ the piano.	☐	☐
4. I really hate to _____ homework on weekends.	☐	☐
5. I rarely _____ basketball.	☐	☐
6. I never _____ gymnastics.	☐	☐
7. I always _____ ski in the winter.	☐	☐
8. I like to _____ running.	☐	☐
9. I love to _____ baseball.	☐	☐

B ▶ Pair work. Work with a partner. Read the statements from activity A that are true for you. After each statement, your partner should ask you a question. Take turns. Write your partner's answers about his or her true statements.

Example: A: I can play the piano.
           B: When did you start taking piano lessons?

1. _____

   _____

2. _____

   _____

3. _____

   _____

4. _____

   _____

5. _____

   _____

6. _____

   _____

7. _____

   _____

8. _____

   _____

9. _____

   _____

A ▶ **Practice.** Complete the sentences with *out* or *over*.

1. My wife and I like to eat _____ once a week.

2. John can't figure _____ that math problem.

3. I can't answer your questions right now. I need some time to think it _____.

4. I have to buy some new pants. I wore _____ my old ones.

5. Do you want to come to the gym? I'm going to work _____.

6. I really like Jean and Joe. I want to have them _____ some evening.

7. She doesn't want to go _____ tonight. She's tired and wants to stay home.

8. I found _____ that my boss is leaving the company. I was really surprised.

B ▶ **Pair work.** Write answers to these questions. Then discuss them with a partner.

1. When you go out, where do you like to go for fun? _____

_____

_____

2. What subject in school is the most difficult for you to figure out? What is difficult about it? _____

_____

_____

3. Describe the last time you found out something surprising. _____

_____

_____

4. Do you like to work out? Why or why not? _____

_____

_____

5. Do you usually have people over or do you eat out? _____

_____

_____

6. Do you wear out your clothes quickly? _____

_____

_____

A ▶ Rewrite. Change the phrases in bold to a word or phrase from the box.

an acquaintance	participants	a stranger
information	some research	sender

1. The scientists did **an investigation** about that disease last year.

_____

2. **Someone I know** told me that there was a big problem at that company.

_____

3. The **people who took part** in that study received a payment of $1,000 from the scientists.

_____

4. He sent me some **facts** about that product.

_____

5. **Someone I don't know** sent me a long letter asking for money.

_____

6. The **person who sent me that email** is a close friend of mine.

_____

B ▶ Count and noncount nouns. Complete the sentences with *a little* or *a few*.

1. We have _____ acquaintances in this town.
2. There are _____ strangers in this crowd, but I know almost everyone.
3. I have _____ time today to work on that project.
4. _____ participants in that medical study were cured of their disease.
5. We're starting to do _____ research on email problems.
6. I have only _____ information about that job.

A ▶ Matching. Match each word or phrase with its definition.

1. ____ livable
2. ____ climate
3. ____ culture
4. ____ art galleries
5. ____ sophisticated
6. ____ residents

a. artistic and intellectual activity in a city
b. easy to live in
c. people who live in a place
d. refined, worldly, or complex
e. the general weather conditions
f. shops that sell paintings, photographs, and sculptures

B ▶ Group discussion. Write answers to these questions. Then discuss them in small groups.

1. What makes a city livable? List at least five factors. _____

_____

_____

2. What is the climate like in your city? Give details about the different seasons. _____

_____

_____

_____

3. Is there a lot of culture in your city? Describe the artistic and intellectual life there. _____

_____

_____

_____

4. Do you like to go to art galleries and art museums? Which ones do you like to visit? _____

_____

_____

_____

5. Give an example of a sophisticated person you know. What makes that person sophisticated? _____

_____

_____

_____

6. Describe the residents of your city. Give at least five adjectives to describe them. _____

_____

_____

_____

A ▶ Practice. Check (✓) the correct compound word.

1. ____ air line   ____ airline   ____ air-line
2. ____ business man   ____ businessman   ____ business-man
3. ____ crew members   ____ crewmembers   ____ crew-members
4. ____ dare devil   ____ daredevil   ____ dare-devil
5. ____ hot air balloon ____ hotair balloon   ____ hot-air balloon
6. ____ outer space   ____ outerspace   ____ outer-space
7. ____ space travel   ____ spacetravel   ____ space-travel
8. ____ space ship   ____ spaceship   ____ space-ship

B ▶ Discussion. Read each statement and check (✓) whether you agree or disagree. Write reasons for your opinions. Then discuss your opinions with your class.

1. In 50 years, airline companies will be flying to space hotels.

   ____ I agree.   ____ I disagree.

   _____

   _____

2. I would like to go up in a hot-air balloon.

   ____ I agree.   ____ I disagree.

   _____

   _____

3. In the future, businesspeople will build better spaceships than governments.

   ____ I agree.   ____ I disagree.

   _____

   _____

4. I would like to go into outer space.

   ____ I agree.   ____ I disagree.

   _____

   _____

5. I am a daredevil.

   ____ I agree.   ____ I disagree.

   _____

   _____

A ▶ Practice.   Complete the sentences with words from the box.

device	increase	particular	signal
expectations	moderate	severe	weak

1. If you think that you are badly hurt, the pain will _____.

2. I'm very sick with a cold. I feel very _____.

3. A broken bone can cause _____ pain. You may need to take pain medication.

4. I'm very careful to buy only the best bread. I go to a _____ bakery that always has excellent bread.

5. The spaceship sent a radio _____ back to the Earth.

6. I'm feeling _____ pain on my back. I got a little sunburn at the beach.

7. This class is different from my _____. I thought that it would be boring, but it's really interesting.

8. An X-ray machine is an important medical _____.

B ▶ Group discussion.   Write answers to these questions. Then discuss them in small groups.

1. What are your expectations for this class? Do you think that you will pass it?

   _____

   _____

2. Describe the last time that you were sick. Did you feel weak? Did you feel moderate or severe pain?

   _____

   _____

3. Give an example of a device that gives off a signal. What is it used for?

   _____

   _____

4. When you shop, do you go to particular stores or do you like to try different stores?

   _____

   _____

5. What is increasing in your life? Give several examples.

   _____

   _____

A ▶ Crossword puzzle. Complete the crossword. It includes vocabulary words from Unit 12 and from other units.

ACROSS

1. Martin never makes any noise. He is
   _____.
3. a machine that takes people away from the Earth
6. the opposite of *unable*
7. the opposite of *shy*
8. the opposite of "strong"
9. Mila can play the piano and the flute. She is a _____ musician.
11. smart
12. Can you _____ the piano?
13. Your fingers touch this part of a computer
14. Scientists do this; a kind of study
15. In this sport, you hit other people with big gloves

DOWN

2. John isn't needy. He works well by himself. He's very _____.
3. the opposite of failure
4. Sam thinks carefully about everything. He is a _____ man.
5. Jenny really wants to succeed. She is very _____.
10. a company that flies airplanes

A ▶ Practice. Complete the letter with words from the box.

choir	encouraged	talented	unknown
competition	professional	turning point	

Max Wilkins came from a very poor family. His family loved music. His father sang and his mother played piano. When Max was 10 years old, he started singing in the _____ at his church. His
1
friends heard his singing and loved it! They said that he was a very _____ singer. His friends
2
_____ him to sing at local events. There was a big music _____. The prize was $1,000.
3   4
Max decided to enter it. Max won the $1,000 and became a _____ singer. No one outside his town
5
knew him. He was still _____. The contest was still a _____ in his life, however. Max
6   7
went to college and became an excellent music teacher in his old high school.

B ▶ Discussion. Write answers to these questions. Then discuss them in small groups.

1. Who is the most talented person you know? Why do you think that person is the most talented?

   _____

   _____

2. Would you like to sing in a choir? Why or why not?

   _____

   _____

3. In your life, who encourages you now or encouraged you in the past?

   _____

   _____

4. Give some examples of people who are professionals.

   _____

   _____

5. What competitions do you know about? Give several examples.

   _____

   _____

6. Was there a turning point in your life? Explain.

   _____

   _____

GRAMMAR REFERENCE

UNIT 1

A ▶ The Simple Present of *Be*

Affirmative Statements

I	am	a student.
You	are	a student.
He	is	a student.
She	is	a student.
It	is	a movie.
We	are	students.
You	are	students.
They	are	students.

Negative Statements

I	am not	a teacher.
You	are not	a teacher.
He	is not	a teacher.
She	is not	a teacher.
It	is not	a movie.
We	are not	teachers.
You	are not	teachers.
They	are not	teachers.

Yes-No Questions

Am	I	a student?
Are	you	a student?
Is	he	a student?
Is	she	a student?
Is	it	a movie?
Are	we	students?
Are	you	students?
Are	they	students?

Wh-Questions

What is your major?
Where are you a student?
How old are you?
Why are you a student there?
Who is your teacher?
When is your class?
What time is your class?
Where are we going?

B ▶ The Simple Present of Other Verbs

Affirmative Statements

I	play	
You	play	
He	plays	
She	plays	music.
It	plays	
We	play	
You	play	
They	play	

Negative Statements

I	don't play	
You	don't play	
He	doesn't play	
She	doesn't play	music.
It	doesn't play	
We	don't play	
You	don't play	
They	don't play	

Yes-No Questions

Do	I		
Do	you		
Does	he		
Does	she	play	music?
Does	it		
Do	we		
Do	you		
Do	they		

Wh-Questions

What does he study?
Where do you go on Saturday?
What kind of movies do you like?
Why do you watch horror movies?
Who teaches you English?
When do we leave?
What time does the bus come?

UNIT 4

A ▶ The Simple Past of *Be*

Affirmative Statements

I	was	
You	were	
He	was	
She	was	cold yesterday.
It	was	
We	were	
You	were	
They	were	

Negative Statements

I	wasn't	
You	weren't	
He	wasn't	
She	wasn't	cold yesterday.
It	wasn't	
We	weren't	
You	weren't	
They	weren't	

Yes-No Questions

Was	I		
Were	you		
Was	he		
Was	she	cold	yesterday?
Was	it		
Were	we		
Were	you		
Were	they		

Wh-Questions

Where	was	I?
Where	were	you?
How	was	he?
Who	was	she?
What	was	it?
How	were	you?
When	were	they?

B ▶ The Simple Past of Other Verbs

Affirmative Statements		
I You He She It We You They	worked	yesterday.

Negative Statements		
I You He She It We You They	didn't work	yesterday.

Yes-No Questions			
Did	I you he she it we you they	work	yesterday?

Wh-Questions			
What Where When How Why What time How much	did	I you he she we you they	do yesterday? work? work? work yesterday? work yesterday? work yesterday? work yesterday?

C ▶ Irregular Verbs—Simple Past Forms and Past Participles

Base Form	Simple Past	Past Participle	Base Form	Simple Past	Past Participle
be	was/were	been	keep	kept	kept
become	became	become	know	knew	known
begin	began	begun	leave	left	left
bleed	bled	bled	lend	lent	lent
break	broke	broken	lose	lost	lost
bring	brought	brought	make	made	made
buy	bought	bought	meet	met	met
choose	chose	chosen	pay	paid	paid
come	came	come	put	put	put
cost	cost	cost	read	read	read
cut	cut	cut	ring	rang	rung
do	did	done	run	ran	run
drink	drank	drunk	see	saw	seen
drive	drove	driven	sell	sold	sold
eat	ate	eaten	send	sent	sent
fall	fell	fallen	set	set	set
feel	felt	felt	shake	shook	shaken
fight	fought	fought	shut	shut	shut
find	found	found	sleep	slept	slept
forget	forgot	forgot	speak	spoke	spoken
fry	fried	fried	speed	sped	sped
get	got	gotten	spend	spent	spent
give	gave	given	take	took	taken
go	went	gone	teach	taught	taught
grow	grew	grown	tell	told	told
have/has	had	had	think	thought	thought
hear	heard	heard	wear	wore	worn
hold	held	held	write	wrote	written
hurt	hurt	hurt			

Comparative and Superlative Forms of Common Adjectives

Adjective	Comparative	Superlative
bad	worse than	the worst
beautiful	more beautiful than	the most beautiful
big	bigger than	the biggest
boring	more boring than	the most boring
busy	busier than	the busiest
crazy	crazier than	the craziest
difficult	more difficult than	the most difficult
easy	easier than	the easiest
famous	more famous than	the most famous
far	farther/further than	the farthest/furthest
flat	flatter than	the flattest
funny	funnier than	the funniest
good	better than	the best
happy	happier than	the happiest
heavy	heavier than	the heaviest
hot	hotter than	the hottest
intelligent	more intelligent than	the most intelligent
nice	nicer than	the nicest
sad	sadder than	the saddest
safe	safer than	the safest
strong	stronger than	the strongest
tall	taller than	the tallest

UNIT 8

A ▶ The Present Continuous

Affirmative Statements	
I	am working.
You	are working.
He	is working.
She	is working.
It	is working.
We	are working
You	are working.
They	are working.

Negative Statements	
I	am not working.
You	aren't working.
He	isn't working.
She	isn't working.
It	isn't working.
We	aren't working.
You	aren't working.
They	aren't working.

Yes-No Questions		
Am	I	
Are	you	
Is	he	
Is	she	working?
Is	it	
Are	we	
Are	you	
Are	they	

Wh-Questions		
When	am I	
Where	are you	
Why	is he	
How	is she	working?
What time	are we	
How much	are you	
How often	are they	

B ▶ Spelling Rules for Verbs with -*ing* and -*ed*

Verbs with One Syllable
- If the verb ends in a consonant-vowel-consonant pattern (C-V-C), double the final consonant and add –*ed* or -*ing*.
- If the verb ends in a vowel-vowel-consonant pattern (V-V-C), add –*ed* or –*ing*.

stop—stopped
rub—rubbing
rain—rained
speak—speaking

Verbs with Two Syllables
- If the first syllable is stressed, add the –*ed* or –*ing* ending.
- For verbs in which the second syllable is stressed, double the final consonant.

offer—offering

refer—referring

Verbs ending in -*y*
- If the verb ends in a consonant and -*y*, change the -*y* to -*i* and add –*ed* or –*ing*.
- If the verb ends in a vowel and -*y*, add –*ed*, or –*ing*.

study—studied
play—played

Verbs Ending in a Consonant and –*e*
- If the verb ends in –*e*, just add –*d*.
- If the verb ends in –*e*, drop the –*e* and add –*ing*.

dance—danced
dance—dancing

Verbs Ending in –*ie*
- If the verb ends in –*ie*, add –*d*.
- If the verb ends in –*ie*, change the –*ie* to –*y*, and add –*ing*.

die—died
die—dying

NOTE: Don't double the consonants for words ending in –*w*, -*x*, –*y*.

fix—fixed
allow—allowing
enjoy—enjoying

UNIT 10

Be Going to for Future Plans and Intentions

I	am going to		I	am not going to	
You	are going to		You	aren't going to	
He	is going to		He	isn't going to	
She	is going to	leave tomorrow.	She	isn't going to	be here tomorrow.
It	is going to		It	isn't going to	
We	are going to		We	aren't going to	
You	are going to		You	aren't going to	
They	are going to		They	aren't going to	

UNIT 12

The Present Perfect

Affirmative Statements				**Negative Statements**		
I	have			I	have not	
You	have			You	have not	
He	has			He	has not	
She	has	been here for 3 hours.		She	has not	left yet.
It	has	been here since yesterday.		It	has not	
We	have			We	have not	
You	have			You	have not	
They	have			They	have not	

VOCABULARY SUMMARY

Unit 1

action movies (*n phrase*)
classical (*adj*)
comedies (*n*)
favorite food (*n phrase*)
favorite kind of movie (*n phrase*)
favorite kind of music (*n phrase*)
hip hop (*n phrase*)
horror movies (*n phrase*)
interests (*n*)
jazz (*n*)
pop (*n*)
rap (*n*)
rock (*n*)
romantic movies (*n phrase*)

Unit 2

get a lot of sleep (*v phrase*)
get exercise (*v phrase*)
get stressed out (*v phrase*)
go on a picnic (*v phrase*)
go to the movies (*v phrase*)
take a vacation (*v phrase*)
take night classes (*v phrase*)
take vitamins (*v phrase*)

Unit 3

amusement park (*n phrase*)
bank (*n*)
café (*n*)
campus (*n*)
club (*n*)
doctor's office (*n phrase*)
gym (*n*)
mall (*n*)
park (*n*)
restaurant (*n*)
subway station (*n phrase*)
theater (*n*)

Expansion Units 1–3

eat at a restaurant (*v phrase*)
get fresh air (*v phrase*)
get some exercise (*v phrase*)
go ice-skating (*v phrase*)
go skiing (*v phrase*)
go snowboarding (*v phrase*)
go swimming (*v phrase*)
have a picnic (*v phrase*)
listen to the ocean (*v phrase*)

play volleyball (*v phrase*)
relax in the sand (*v phrase*)
sunbathe at the beach (*v phrase*)
talk with friends (*v phrase*)

Unit 4

book (*n*)
boring (*adj*)
come across (*phrasal verb*)
discover (*v*)
exciting (*adj*)
fascinating (*adj*)
find (*v*)
hoax (*n*)
interesting (*adj*)
joke (*n*)
mysterious (*adj*)
strange (*adj*)
tell (*v*)
trick (*n*)
uncomfortable (*adj*)
unusual (*adj*)

Unit 5

be crazy about (*expression*)
be here to stay (*expression*)
be worth every penny (*expression*)
cost an arm and a leg (*expression*)
give someone the creeps (*expression*)
take off (*phrasal verb*)
turn down (*phrasal verb*)

Unit 6

cell phone (*n*)
display (*v*)
go online (*v*)
keyboard (*n*)
recharge (*v*)
screen (*n*)
surf (*v*)
text message (*n phrase*)
website (*n*)

Expansion Units 4–6

all the rage (*adj phrase*)
ghost (*n*)
made a fortune (*v phrase*)
materials (*n*)
tent (*n*)
wear out (*phrasal verb*)

Unit 7

box *(v)*
do gymnastics *(v phrase)*
do homework *(v phrase)*
go golfing *(v phrase)*
go horseback riding *(v phrase)*
go jogging *(v phrase)*
go running *(v phrase)*
go skiing *(v phrase)*
go surfing *(v phrase)*
go swimming *(v phrase)*
golf *(v)*
jog *(v)*
play baseball *(phrase)*
play basketball *(v phrase)*
play golf *(v phrase)*
play soccer *(v phrase)*
play tennis *(v phrase)*
play the drums *(v phrase)*
play the guitar *(v phrase)*
play the piano *(v phrase)*
play volleyball *(v phrase)*
run *(v)*
ski *(v)*
surf *(v)*
swim *(v)*

Unit 8

eat out *(phrasal verb)*
figure out *(phrasal verb)*
find out *(phrasal verb)*
go out *(phrasal verb)*
have over *(phrasal verb)*
think over *(phrasal verb)*
wear out *(phrasal verb)*
work out *(phrasal verb)*

Unit 9

acquaintance *(n)*
information *(n)*
news *(n)*
participant *(n)*
research *(n)*
sender *(n)*
stranger *(n)*
study *(n)*
time *(n)*
work *(n)*

Expansion Units 7–9

art galleries *(n phrase)*
climate *(n)*
culture *(n)*
livable *(adj)*
residents *(n)*
sophisticated *(adj)*

Unit 10

airline *(n)*
businessman *(n)*
crew members *(n phrase)*
daredevil *(n)*
hot-air balloon *(n phrase)*
outer space *(n phrase)*
space travel *(n phrase)*
spaceship *(n)*

Unit 11

device *(n)*
expectations *(n)*
increase *(v)*
moderate *(adj)*
particular *(adj)*
severe *(adj)*
signal *(n)*
weak *(adj)*

Unit 12

capable *(adj)*
independent *(adj)*
intelligent *(adj)*
motivated *(adj)*
outgoing *(adj)*
quiet *(adj)*
talented *(adj)*
thoughtful *(adj)*

Expansion Units 10–12

choir *(n)*
competition *(n)*
encouraged *(v)*
professional *(adj)*
talented *(adj)*
turning point *(n phrase)*
unknown *(adj)*

Critical Thinking

Brainstorming Ideas, 6, 25, 46, 63, 64, 69, 72, 85, 90, 98
Categorizing, 25, 27, 28, 42,
Comparing and Contrasting, 9, 13, 19, 45, 83, 90
Getting Meaning from Context, 67, 84
Identifying Advantages and Disadvantages (pros and cons), 25, 62, 93,
Identifying Main Ideas, 10, 16, 18, 28, 30, 37, 44, 45, 52, 53, 57, 64, 66, 80, 81, 93, 100, 102, 112
Identifying Problems and Solutions, 53
Identifying Supporting Examples, 64, 73, 81
Integrating Information from Multiple Sources, 9, 17, 25, 37, 45, 53, 65, 73
Interpreting Graphs to Help Comprehension, 58, 65
Making Inferences, 14, 17, 22, 53, 54, 70, 74, 82, 83, 101, 102, 106, 111
Opinions
  Distinguishing Fact from Opinion, 39
  Identifying Information that Contradicts an Opinion, 65
  Identifying Reasons that Support an Opinion, 80, 81
  Supporting an Opinion with Reasons, 80, 85
Predictions
  Identifying Predictions, 37
  Making Predictions, 22, 30, 34, 37, 38, 56, 90, 106
Ranking, 37, 58, 59, 83, 85, 90, 94
Recognizing Cause and Effect, 109
Sequencing, 31, 34, 36, 45, 55, 75, 98
Summarizing, 47, 50, 52, 110
Using Graphic Organizers
  Mind Maps, 64, 85
  T-Charts, 25
  Venn Diagrams, 19, 28, 90

Grammar

Adverbs of Frequency and Time Expressions, 12, 13
Comparative and Superlative Forms of Adjectives, 60, 61, 83
Demonstrative Adjectives and Pronouns, 40, 41
Expressing Future Plans and Intentions with *Be Going to*, 88, 89
Expressions of Quantity, 76, 77
Infinitives, 96, 97
Present Continuous, 68, 69
Present Perfect, 104, 105
Simple Past: Statements, Negatives, Questions, 32, 33
Simple Present: Statements, Negatives, Questions, 4, 5
Modals of Ability, 48, 49
Using *there is* and *there are* with *some* and *any*, 20, 21

Listening

Categorizing, 27, 42
Comparing and Contrasting, 45, 90
Identifying Advantages and Disadvantages, 62, 93
Identifying Problems and Solutions, 53
Listening for Frequency, 13, 14, 26, 27
Listening for General Information, 6, 14, 25, 53, 65, 73, 78, 81, 109
Listening for Gist, 70, 101
Listening for Specific Information, 4, 6, 9, 13, 14, 17, 20, 22, 25, 26, 27, 28, 33, 34, 37, 41, 42, 50 53, 54 61, 62, 65, 69, 70, 73, 77, 78, 81, 83, 89, 90, 93, 97, 98, 101, 105, 106, 109, 111
Listening for Time Expressions, 42
Making Inferences, 14, 17, 22, 53, 77, 83, 101, 111
Making Predictions, 22, 34, 50, 90
Opinions
  Identifying Opinions, 93
  Listening for Details that Support an Opinion, 83
  Listening for Reasons that Support an Opinion, 93
Recognizing Tone, 62, 83
Sequencing, 34, 45, 55, 98
Summarizing, 50, 106, 110

Reading

Choosing the Best Title or Heading, 17, 95, 109, 113
Comparing and Contrasting, 19, 45, 90
Distinguishing Fact from Opinion, 39
Getting Meaning from Context, 67, 84
Identifying Abilities, 49
Identifying Details, 52, 57, 72, 92, 100
Identifying Goals and Steps to Accomplish Them, 108, 113
Identifying Problems and Solutions, 53, 81, 101
Identifying Supporting Examples, 64, 81, 85
Identifying Topic Sentences, 16, 100
Interpreting Graphs to Help Comprehension, 58, 65
Making Inferences, 17, 53, 54, 74, 82, 101, 102, 106
Making Predictions, 30, 37, 38, 56
Main Ideas
  Skimming to Identify the Main Idea, 10, 16, 18, 28, 44, 45, 52, 53, 57, 64, 80, 81, 85, 93, 100, 101, 102, 112
Opinions
  Distinguishing Fact from Opinion, 39
  Identifying Opinions, 81, 93
  Identifying Supporting Reasons for an Opinion, 80, 93
Paraphrasing, 87, 92, 113

Reading for Specific Information, 3, 8, 17, 21, 37, 44, 45, 49, 52, 53, 57, 59, 64, 65, 72, 73, 80, 81, 82, 83, 85, 92, 93, 100, 101, 103, 108, 109, 111, 112, 113

Scanning for Specific Information, 2, 5, 9, 11, 19, 21, 24, 25, 29, 36, 46, 58, 65, 84, 86

Sequencing, 31, 36, 45, 75

Skimming for Topic and Overview, 16, 17, 30, 37, 56, 58, 66, 73, 74, 94, 100, 102, 109

Summarizing, 47, 52, 57

Understanding Point of View, 102, 103

Using Headings to Aid Comprehension, 95

Speaking and Conversation Strategies

Asking and Answering Frequency Questions, 14, 26, 27, 42, 76

Asking for Additional Information, 23

Asking for and Giving Advice, 107

Asking for and Giving Personal Information, 2, 3, 26, 27, 29, 33, 34, 42, 61, 97, 101, 102, 105, 106, 110, 113

Asking for and Giving Recommendations, 91, 111

Asking for Clarification, 7

Asking for Permission, 71

Brainstorming Ideas, 6, 46, 51, 59, 63, 69, 90, 98

Describing Favorites, 21

Explaining a Process, 99

Expressing Disbelief, 25

Expressing Excitement and Enthusiasm, 63

Giving Reasons, 87

Invitations: Offering, Accepting, and Declining, 51

Making Requests, 71

Opinions
    Asking for and Giving Opinions, 22, 23, 25, 29, 31, 37, 39, 43, 47, 55, 67, 69, 73, 79, 85, 86, 95, 103, 111
    Expressing Similar and Different Opinions, 43

Ranking, 90

Role-playing, 7, 15, 35, 40, 51, 71, 96, 99

Sequencing, 50, 55

Showing Interest, 15

Talking about Ability, 49, 50

Vocabulary

Antonyms, 103

Compound Nouns, 87

Count and Noncount Nouns, 75

Guessing the Meaning of Words in Context, 56, 67, 84, 95, 112

Interpreting Idioms, 39

Phrasal Verbs, 67

Using Synonyms, 31

Using Technological Vocabulary, 47

Using Phrases for Sports with *do*, *go*, and *play*, 59

Using Phrases with *get*, *take*, and *go*, 11

Vocabulary Categories (recognizing), 3, 19

Writing

Brainstorming Ideas, 8, 24, 25, 36, 64, 72, 85

Identifying Advantages and Disadvantages, 62

Identifying Goals and Steps to Accomplish them, 108

Opinions
    Using Examples to Support an Opinion, 64, 85
    Supporting an Opinion with Reasons, 80, 85

Organizing Ideas Using Graphic Organizers
    Mind Maps, 64, 85
    Outline, 108
    Venn diagrams, 28, 90

Paraphrasing, 92

Summarizing, 52

Using Connecting Words, 24

Using Supporting Details, 72, 100

Using Time Words to Sequence Events, 36

Writing Concluding Sentences, 44, 57

Writing Statements and Questions, 8, 29

Writing Topic Sentences, 16, 72, 100, 108